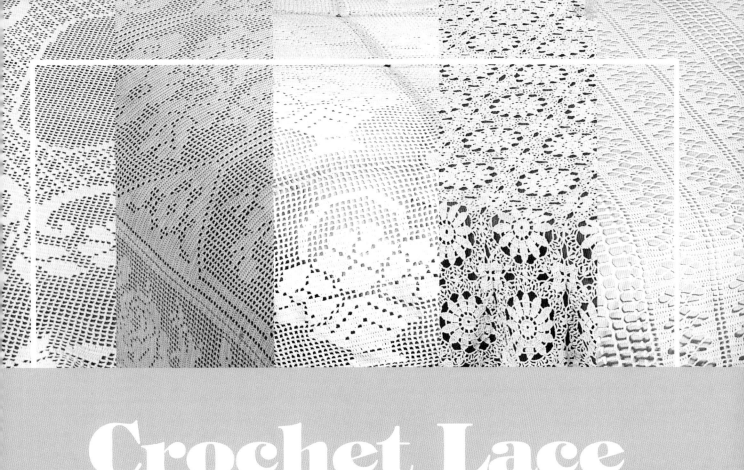

Crochet Lace

Jean Leinhauser & Rita Weiss

STERLING

New York / London
www.sterlingpublishing.com

STERLING and the distinctive Sterling logo are registered trademarks of Sterling Publishing Co., Inc.

Library of Congress Cataloging-in-Publication Data Available

10 9 8 7 6 5 4 3 2 1

Published by Sterling Publishing Co., Inc.
387 Park Avenue South, New York, NY 10016

© 2008 by The Creative Partners™ LLC

Production Team
    Creative Directors:
      Jean Leinhauser
      Rita Weiss

    Editor:
      Susan Lowman

    Photography:
      Carol Mansfield

    Book Design:
      Joyce Lerner

Distributed in Canada by Sterling Publishing
c/o Canadian Manda Group, 165 Dufferin Street,
Toronto, Ontario, Canada M6K 3H6

Distributed in the United Kingdom by GMC Distribution Services,
Castle Place, 166 High Street, Lewes, East Sussex, England BN7 1XU

Distributed in Australia by Capricorn Link (Australia) Pty. Ltd.
P.O. Box 704, Windsor, NSW 2756, Australia

Printed in China

Sterling ISBN-13: 978-1-4027-3350-5
       ISBN-10: 1-4027-3350-X

For information about custom editions, special sales, premium and corporate purchases, please contact Sterling Special Sales Department at 800-805-5489 or specialsales@sterlingpublishing.com.

INTRODUCTION

We found them at garage sales, at swap meets, at resale shops, and a few at antique shows. We were both rescuing vintage pieces of crochet long before we knew each other. We've combined the best of our collections to create this book.

Each of them was made many years ago, probably cherished for a time, then finally cast off. No one else seemed to want them, but we did!

We don't know who made these exquisite bedspreads and tablecloths, and except in one case, we don't know who designed them. But these anonymous crocheters will now always have a place in the historical archives of crochet.

These magnificent examples of the crocheter's art can come to life again with your skill and love, because technical editor Susan Lowman has spent countless hours figuring out how they were made, and writing patterns for them.

Some of them were crocheted with finer threads than we would use today, so the patterns have been written with that in mind.

These wonderful projects aren't designed to be made in a weekend. They will take time, but the result will be something that will become an heirloom for your family, bringing beauty and remembrance of the past to generations to come.

Meanwhile we will continue to bring out these and others from our collections to celebrate a special dinner, or to welcome friends to our guest rooms.

Jean Leinhauser
Rita Weiss
Creative Partners™, LLC

CONTENTS

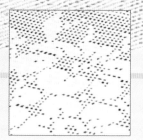

Signs of Spring
6

Spider Wheel
Tablecloth
14

Lacy Panels
Bedspread
18

Elegant Pineapples
Tablecloth
22

Peackock Filet
Bedspread
28

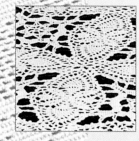

Pineapple Ovals
Tablecloth
36

Filet
Flower Baskets
Bedroom Set
42

Flower Circles
Tablecloth
48

Floral Strips
Bedspread
52

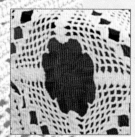

Colorful Floral
Squares
56

Popcorn Diamonds
Bedspread
60

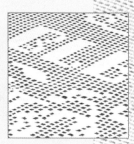

God Bless Our Home Tablecloth 66

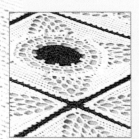

Elegance Bedspread 70

Oval Filet Tablecloth 76

Rosy Table Topper 80

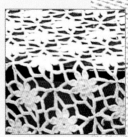

Daisy Filigree Tablecloth 86

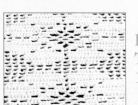

Harvest Cloth 90

Frosty Pineapples Bedspread 96

Floral Medallions Tablecloth 102

Adjustable Size Pineapple Tablecloth 106

Butterfly Filet Table Topper 110

Elegance for the Table 116

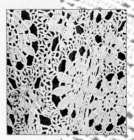

Animals on Parade Child's Spread 120

General Directions 132

Index 144

Signs of Spring

The first birds of spring and early blossoms are the theme for this lovely filet bedspread, worked in blocks. Each individual block would make a lovely framed picture.

SIZE: 76" x 86" plus fringe

MATERIALS

Size 10 crochet cotton,
49 balls (400 yds each) or 19,600 yds white
Size 7 (1.65 mm) steel crochet hook
 (or size required for gauge)

GAUGE

14 mesh = 4"; 15 mesh rows = 4"

SPECIAL STITCHES

Popcorn (PC): Work 5 dc in specified st or sp, remove lp from hook, insert hook from front to back in top of first of 5 dc, return lp to hook and pull lp through first dc: PC made.

Note: *Work all dc in front lp only.*

Instructions

CENTER MOTIFS

(make 4 of Motif 1, 2 of Motif 2, 2 of Motif 3 and 1 of Motif 4)

Ch 201.

Row (right side)1: Dc in 9th ch from hook; *ch 2, skip next 2 chs, dc in next ch; rep from * across: 65 open mesh; ch 5, turn.

Rows 2 through 79 (89): Work open and closed mesh as per Motif Charts 1 through 4 and filet instructions on pages 134-138. At end of last row, finish off; weave in ends.

Note: *Motifs 1 and 2 have 79 rows. Motifs 3 and 4 have 89 rows.*

TOP AND BOTTOM EDGING STRIPS
(make 2)

Ch 102.

Row 1 (right side): Dc in 9th ch from hook; *ch 2, skip next 2 chs, dc in next ch; rep from * across: 32 open mesh; ch 5, turn.

Rows 2 through 99: Work open and closed mesh as per Edging chart and filet instructions on pages 134-138.

Rows 100 through 195: Rep Rows 4 through 99 on chart. At end of Row 195, finish off; weave in ends.

RIGHT BORDER

Row 1: With right side of Top Edging Strip facing, join with sl st in 6th skipped ch at beg of Row 1 at bottom right-hand corner, ch 5 (counts as dc and ch-2 sp), dc in 3rd skipped ch at beg of Row 1; *PC around post of last dc on next row, ch 1, dc in top of same dc, ch 2, dc in 3rd ch of turning ch-5 on next row; rep from * across to top right-hand corner: 97 PC and 98 ch-2 sps. Finish off; weave in ends.

Row 2: With right side facing, join with sl st in 3rd ch of beg ch-5 on Row 1 of Border, ch 3, PC in first ch-2 sp, ch 1, dc in next dc; *ch 2, skip next PC, dc in next dc, PC in next ch-2 sp, ch 1, dc in next dc; rep from * across: 98 PC and 97 ch-2 sps. Finish off; weave in ends.

Rep Right Border on Bottom Edging Strip.

LEFT BORDER

Row 1: With right side of Top Edging Strip facing, join with sl st in top of last dc on Row 195 at top left-hand corner, ch 5 (counts as dc and ch-2 sp), dc in 3rd ch of turning ch-5 on next row; *PC in ch-sp at edge of same row, ch 1, dc in top of last dc on next row, ch 2, dc in 3rd ch of turning ch-5 on next row; rep from * across to bottom left-hand corner, working final dc in first ch of foundation ch: 97 PC and 98 ch-2 sps. Finish off; weave in ends.

Row 2: Rep Row 2 on Right Border.

Rep Left Border on Bottom Edging Strip.

SIDE EDGING STRIPS
(make 2)

Ch 102.

Row 1 *(right side)*: Work same as Row 1 on Top and Bottom Edging Strips.

Row 2: Skip first dc, dc in next dc; *ch 2, skip next 2 chs, dc in next dc; rep from * across: 32 open mesh; ch 5, turn.

Rows 3 and 4: Rep Row 2 two times more.

Rows 5 through 103: Work open and closed mesh as per Rows 1 through 99 on Edging chart and filet instructions on pages 134-138.

Rows 104 through 108: Rep Row 2 five times more.

Rows 109 through 207: Rep Rows 5 through 103 (Rows 1 through 99 on Edging chart).

Rows 208 through 311: Rep Rows 104 through 207.

Rows 312 through 315: Rep Row 2 four times more. At end of Row 315, finish off; weave in ends.

BORDER
(work on both Side Edging Strips)

Rnd 1: With right side facing, join with sl st in 6th skipped ch at beg of Row 1 at bottom right-hand corner, ch 3 (counts as dc), working across right-hand edge, PC in ch-sp at edge of Row 1, ch 1, dc in 3rd skipped ch at beg of Row 1 (at base of last dc on Row 2); *ch 2, dc in top of last dc on next row, PC in ch-sp at edge of next row, ch 1, dc in 3rd ch of turning ch-5 on same row; rep from * across to top right-hand corner; working across top edge, ch 5, dc in same ch as last dc, PC in turning ch-5 sp, ch 1, dc in next dc; **ch 2, skip next ch-2 sp, dc in next dc, PC in next ch-2 sp, ch 1, dc in next dc; rep from ** across to last ch-2 sp at next corner; ch 2, skip last ch-2 sp, dc in last dc; working across left-hand edge, ch 3, PC around post of last dc made, ch 1, dc in last dc on Row 315; ***ch 2, dc in 3rd ch of turning ch-5 on next row, PC in ch-sp on same row, ch 1, dc in top of last dc on next row; rep from *** across to Row 1; ch 2, dc in first ch of foundation ch (at base of last dc on Row 1); working across bottom edge, ch 3, PC around post of last dc made, ch 1, dc in first ch of foundation ch; ****ch 2, skip next 2 chs, dc in next ch (at base of next dc on Row 1), PC in next ch-2 sp, ch 1, dc in ch at base of next dc on Row 1; rep from **** across to bottom right-hand corner, working last dc in same ch as joining; ch 2, dc in 3rd ch of beg ch-3: 349 PC and 349 ch-2 sps.

Rnd 2: Ch 3, PC around post of last dc on Rnd 1, ch 1, dc in 3rd ch of beg ch-3 on Rnd 1; *ch 2, skip next PC, dc in next dc, PC in next ch-2 sp, ch 1, dc in next dc*; rep from * to * across to next corner, working last PC in corner ch-5 sp and last dc in 3rd ch of corner ch-5; ch 5, dc in same ch as last dc, PC in same ch-5 sp, ch 1, dc in next dc; rep from * to * across to next corner; **ch 2, dc in 3rd ch of ch-3 at corner, ch 3, PC around post of last dc made, ch 1, dc in same ch as last dc; rep from * to * across to next corner; rep from * once more; ch 2, dc in 3rd ch of beg ch-3: 353 PC and 353 ch-2 sps. Finish off; weave in ends.

ASSEMBLY

With right sides facing, whip stitch edges of Motifs 1 through 4 together into 3 rows as follows:

Rows 1 and 3—Motif 1, Motif 2, Motif 1

Row 2—Motif 3, Motif 4, Motif 3

Whip stitch assembled rows together. Whip stitch one long edge of Top and Bottom Edging Strips to top and bottom edges of assembled motifs with wings of birds on Edging Strips against assembled motifs. Whip stitch one long edge of Side Edging Strips to left and right edges of assembled motifs with wings of birds on Edging Strips against assembled motifs.

FRINGE

Following Fringe Instructions on page 142, cut 9" long strands of thread. Knot 11 strands in each ch-2 sp around all 4 edges, leaving center of top edge unfringed. Trim if desired.

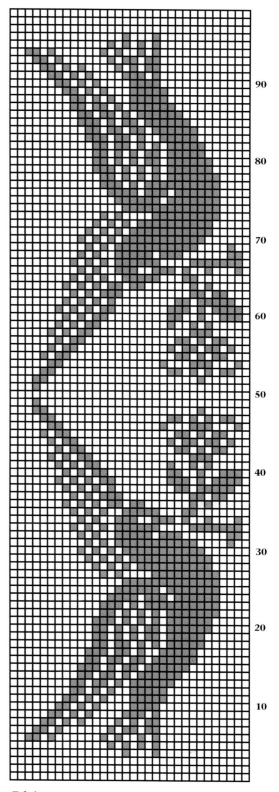

Edgings

KEY
☐ open mesh
■ closed mesh

Motif 1

KEY
☐ open mesh
▨ closed mesh

Motif 2

KEY
□ open mesh
■ closed mesh

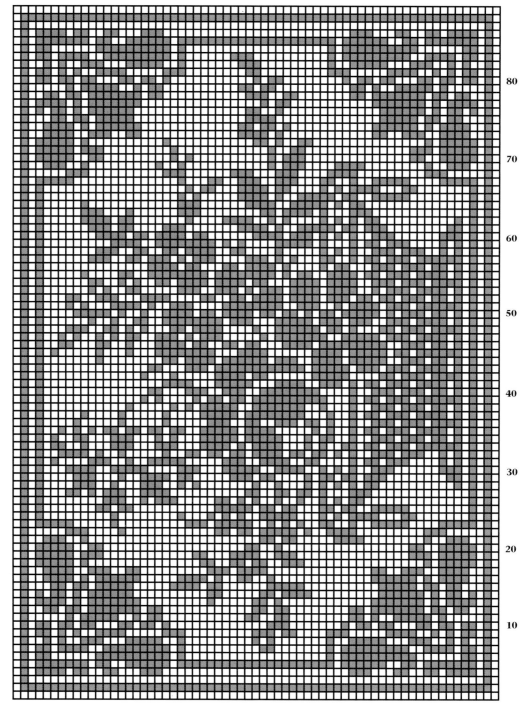

Motif 3

Motif 4

KEY

☐ open mesh

▦ closed mesh

Spider Wheel Tablecloth

Any spider would be proud to weave a web as pretty as the one that forms the motif for this dramatic cloth. Because it is made in motifs, you can adjust the size to fit any table.

SIZE: 30" x 34"

MATERIALS

Size 10 (bedspread weight) crochet thread
7 balls (400 yds each) or 2,800 yds white
Tapestry needle
Size 7 (1.65 mm) steel crochet hook (or size required for gauge)

GAUGE

9-rnd motif = 3³/4" diameter
Rnds 1 through 3 = 1¹/2" diameter

SPECIAL STITCHES

Front Post Extended dc (FP Edc): YO, insert hook from front to back to front around post of specified st and draw up a lp, YO and draw through one lp on hook, (YO and draw through 2 lps on hook) twice: FP Edc made.

Back Post Extended dc (BP Edc): YO, insert hook from back to front to back around post of specified st and draw up a lp, YO and draw through one lp on hook, (YO and draw through 2 lps on hook) twice: BP Edc made.

Instructions

FULL MOTIF
(make 77)

Ch 6; join with sl st to form a ring.

Rnd 1 (right side): Ch 5 (counts as dc and ch-2 sp), (dc in ring, ch 2) 4 times, dc in ring, ch 1; join with hdc in 3rd ch of beg ch-5 (ch 1 and hdc counts as ch-2 sp): 6 dc and 6 ch-2 sps.

Rnd 2: Ch 3 (counts as dc now and throughout), 3 dc around post of hdc, ch 2, (6 dc in next ch-2 sp, ch 2) 5 times, 2 dc in ch-1 sp: 36 dc and 6 ch-2 sps; join with sl st in 3rd ch of beg ch-3.

Rnd 3: Ch 3, dc in next dc; *FP Edc around next 2 dc, ch 3, FP Edc around next 2 dc**, dc in next 2 dc; rep from * 4 times more; rep from * to ** once: 24 FP Edc, 12 dc and 6 ch-3 sps; join as before.

Rnd 4: Ch 3, dc in next dc; *ch 1, FP Edc around next 2 FP Edc, ch 4, FP Edc around next 2 FP Edc, ch 1**, dc in next 2 dc; rep from * 4 times more; rep from * to ** once: 24 FP Edc, 12 dc, 6 ch-4 sps and 12 ch-1 sps; join.

Rnd 5: Sl st in next dc and in next ch-1 sp, ch 3 (counts as dc), dc in same ch-1 sp; *FP Edc around next 2 FP Edc, ch 5, FP Edc around next 2 FP Edc, 2 dc in next ch-1 sp, FP Edc around next 2 dc**, 2 dc in next ch-1 sp; rep from * 4 times more; rep from * to ** once: 36 FP Edc, 24 dc and 6 ch-5 sps; join.

Full motif—front

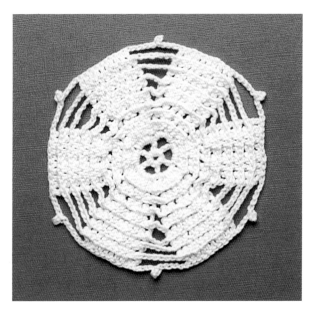

Full motif—back

Rnd 6: Ch 3, dc in next dc; *FP Edc around next 2 FP Edc, ch 6**, (FP Edc around next 2 FP Edc, dc in next 2 dc) 2 times; rep from * 4 times more; rep from * to ** once; FP Edc around next 2 FP Edc, dc in next 2 dc, FP Edc around next 2 FP Edc: 36 FP Edc, 24 dc and 6 ch-6 sps; join.

Rnd 7: Ch 3, dc in next dc; *FP Edc around next 2 FP Edc, ch 7**, (FP Edc around next 2 FP Edc, dc in next 2 dc) 2 times; rep from * 4 times more; rep from * to ** once; FP Edc around next 2 FP Edc, dc in next 2 dc, FP Edc around next 2 FP Edc: 36 FP Edc, 24 dc and 6 ch-7 sps; join.

Rnd 8: Ch 3, dc in next dc; *FP Edc around next 2 FP Edc, ch 8**, (FP Edc around next 2 FP Edc, dc in next 2 dc) 2 times; rep from * 4 times more; rep from * to ** once; FP Edc around next 2 FP Edc, dc in next 2 dc, FP Edc around next 2 FP Edc: 36 FP Edc, 24 dc and 6 ch-8 sps; join.

Rnd 9: Ch 3, dc in next dc; *FP Edc around next 2 FP Edc, ch 8, sl st in 3rd ch from hook (picot made), ch 4**, (FP Edc around next 2 FP Edc, dc in next 2 dc) 2 times; rep from * 4 times more; rep from * to ** once; FP Edc around next 2 FP Edc, dc in next 2 dc, FP Edc around next 2 FP Edc: 36 FP Edc, 24 dc, 6 ch-9 sps and 6 picots; join. Finish off, leaving a 12" end for joining.

HALF MOTIF
(make 8)

Ch 4; join with sl st to form a ring.

Row 1 (right side): Ch 5 (counts as dc and ch-2 sp), (dc in ring, ch 2) 2 times, dc in ring: 4 dc and 3 ch-2 sps; ch 3 (counts as dc on next row now and throughout), turn.

Row 2 (wrong side): (6 dc in next ch-2 sp, ch 2) 2 times, 7 dc in last ch-sp: 20 dc and 2 ch-2 sps; ch 3, turn.

Row 3: Skip first dc; *FP Edc around next 2 dc, dc in next 2 dc, FP Edc around next 2 dc**, ch 3; rep from * once; rep from * to ** once; dc in 3rd ch of turning ch-3: 12 FP Edc, 8 dc and 2 ch-3 sps; ch 3, turn.

Row 4: Skip first dc; *BP Edc around next 2 FP Edc, ch 1, dc in next 2 dc, ch 1, BP Edc around next 2 FP Edc**, ch 4; rep from * once; rep from * to ** once; dc in 3rd ch of turning ch-3: 12 BP Edc, 8 dc, 6 ch-1 sps and 2 ch-4 sps; ch 3, turn.

Row 5: Skip first dc; *FP Edc around next 2 BP Edc, 2 dc in next ch-1 sp, FP Edc around next 2 dc, 2 dc in next ch-1 sp, FP Edc around next 2 BP Edc**, ch 5; rep from * once; rep from * to ** once; dc in 3rd ch of turning ch-3: 18 FP Edc, 14 dc and 2 ch-5 sps; ch 3, turn.

Half motif—front

Half motif—back

Row 6: Skip first dc; *(BP Edc around next 2 FP Edc, dc in next 2 dc) 2 times, BP Edc around next 2 FP Edc**, ch 6; rep from * once; rep from * to ** once; dc in 3rd ch of turning ch-3: 18 BP Edc, 14 dc and 2 ch-6 sps; ch 3, turn.

Row 7: Skip first dc; *(FP Edc around next 2 BP Edc, dc in next 2 dc) 2 times, FP Edc around next 2 BP Edc**, ch 7; rep from * once; rep from * to ** once; dc in 3rd ch of turning ch-3: 18 FP Edc, 14 dc and 2 ch-7 sps; ch 3, turn.

Row 8: Skip first dc; *(BP Edc around next 2 FP Edc, dc in next 2 dc) 2 times, BP Edc around next 2 FP Edc**, ch 8; rep from * once; rep from * to ** once; dc in 3rd ch of turning ch-3: 18 BP Edc, 14 dc and 2 ch-8 sps; ch 3, turn.

Row 9: Skip first dc; *(FP Edc around next 2 BP Edc, dc in next 2 dc) 2 times, FP Edc around next 2 BP Edc**, ch 8, sl st in 3rd ch from hook (picot made), ch 4; rep from * once; rep from * to ** once; dc in 3rd ch of turning ch-3: 18 FP Edc, 14 dc, 2 ch-9 sps and 2 picots. Finish off, leaving a 12" end for joining.

JOINING

Hold 2 motifs with wrong sides tog. With tapestry needle and crochet thread, with overcast st sew motifs tog through back lps of 6 FP Edc and 4 dc between 2 ch-9 sps on one edge of motifs. Join motifs into 5 straight rows of 9 full motifs and 4 straight rows of 8 full motifs with one half motif at each end. Alternate rows and join remaining edges as before to form tablecloth.

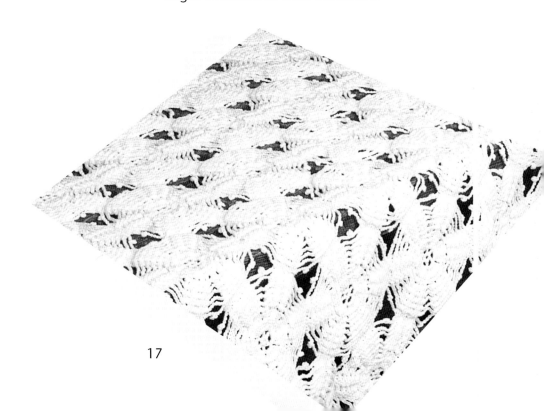

Lacy Panels Bedspread

Easy-to-crochet vertical panels form this pretty spread. The spread can be crocheted to fit any bed because the panels can be adjusted in length and any number of panels can be used to make up the proper width.

SIZE: 84" x 108"

MATERIALS

Size 10 (bedspread weight) crochet thread
25 balls (400 yds each) or 10,000 yds cream
Size 5 steel crochet hook
  (or size required for gauge)

GAUGE

10 dc = 1^1/2"
Rows 1 through 6 = 1^1/2"

Instructions

PANEL
(make 6)

Ch 95.

Row 1 (wrong side): Dc in 8th ch from hook (skipped chs count as dc and ch-2 sp); *ch 2, skip 2 chs, dc in next ch; rep from * across: 31 dc and 30 ch-2 sps; ch 5 (counts as dc and ch-2 sp on next row now and throughout), turn.

Row 2 (right side): Skip first ch-2 sp, dc in next dc; *dc in next 9 sts, (ch 2, skip next ch-2 sp, dc in next dc) 2 times; rep from * 4 times more; dc in next 9 sts, ch 2, skip 2 chs, dc in next ch: 67 dc and 12 ch-2 sps; ch 5, turn.

Row 3: Skip first ch-2 sp, dc in next dc; *dc in next 5 dc, ch 6, skip next 4 dc, sc in next ch-2 sp, ch 4, sc in next ch-2 sp, ch 6, skip next 4 dc, dc in next 6 dc**, (ch 2, skip next ch-2 sp, dc in next dc) 2 times; rep from * once; rep from * to ** once; ch 2, skip next 2 chs, dc in next ch: 40 dc, 6 ch-6 sps, 3 ch-4 sps, 6 ch-2 sps and 6 sc; ch 5, turn.

Row 4: Skip first ch-2 sp, dc in next dc; *dc in next 2 dc, ch 6, skip next 3 dc, sc in next ch-6 sp, ch 1, 4 tr in next ch-4 sp, ch 1, sc in next ch-6 sp, ch 6, skip next 3 dc, dc in next 3 dc**, (ch 2, skip next ch-2 sp, dc in next dc) 2 times; rep from * once; rep from * to ** once; ch 2, skip next 2 chs, dc in next ch: 22 dc, 12 tr, 6 ch-6 sps, 6 ch-2 sps, 6 ch-1 sps and 6 sc; ch 5, turn.

18

Row 5: Skip first ch-2 sp, dc in next dc; *dc in next 2 dc, 3 dc in next ch-6 sp, ch 7, sc between 2nd and 3rd tr, ch 7, 3 dc in next ch-6 sp, dc in next 3 dc**, (ch 2, skip next ch-2 sp, dc in next dc) 2 times; rep from * once; rep from * to ** once; ch 2, skip next 2 chs, dc in next ch: 40 dc, 6 ch-7 sps, 6 ch-2 sps and 3 sc; ch 5, turn.

Row 6: Skip first ch-2 sp, dc in next dc; *dc in next 5 dc, 4 dc in next ch-7 sp, ch 5, 4 dc in next ch-7 sp, dc in next 6 dc**, (ch 2, skip next ch-2 sp, dc in next dc) 2 times; rep from * once; rep from * to ** once; ch 2, skip next 2 chs, dc in next ch: 64 dc, 3 ch-5 sps and 6 ch-2 sps; ch 5, turn.

Row 7: Skip first ch-2 sp, dc in next dc; *dc in next 9 dc, ch 2, sc in next ch-5 sp, ch 2, dc in next 10 dc**, (ch 2, skip next ch-2 sp, dc in next dc) 2 times; rep from * once; rep from * to ** once; ch 2, skip next 2 chs, dc in next ch: 64 dc, 12 ch-2 sps and 3 sc; ch 5, turn.

Rep Rows 3 through 7 sixty eight times more, then rep Rows 3 through 6 once.

Last Row: Skip first ch-2 sp, dc in next dc; *(ch 2, skip 2 dc, dc in next dc) 3 times; ch 2, skip 2 chs, dc in next ch; ch 2, skip 2 chs, dc in next dc; (ch 2, skip 2 dc, dc in next dc) 3 times**; (ch 2, skip 2 chs, dc in next dc) 2 times; rep from * once; rep from * to ** once; ch 2, skip 2 chs, dc in next ch: 31 dc and 30 ch-2 sps. Finish off; weave in ends.

First Panel

Rnd 1: With right side facing, join with sc in first ch sp at bottom left-hand corner of panel, sc in same sp; *(ch 7, sl st in 4th ch from hook, ch 9, sl st in same ch, ch 3, sl st in same ch, ch 3*, 2 sc in same ch sp as last sc made) 2 times; **rep from * to * once; (2 sc in next ch sp) 2 times**; rep from ** to ** across bottom edge to ch sp before corner ch sp; (rep from * to * once; 2 sc in corner ch sp) 3 times; rep from ** to ** across right edge to ch sp before next corner ch sp; rep from * to * once***; 2 sc in corner ch sp; rep from first * to *** across top edge and left edge: 390 ch-9 sps; join with sl st in beg sc. Finish off; weave in ends.

Rnd 2: With right side facing, join with sc in last ch-9 sp; **(ch 7, sc in next ch-9 sp) 3 times in corner; *ch 5, sc in next ch-9 sp; rep from * across to next corner; rep from ** around to beg: 378 ch-5 sps and 12 ch-7 sps; join with sl st in beg sc.

Rnd 3: Ch 1, work (4 sc, ch 4, sl st in top of last sc made, 3 sc) in each corner ch-7 sp and (3 sc, ch 4, sl st in top of last sc made, 2 sc) in each ch-5 sp around: 390 ch-4 sps; join with sl st in beg sc. Finish off; weave in ends.

Second through Sixth Panels

Rnds 1 and 2: Work same as Rnds 1 and 2 of First Panel.

Rnd 3: Ch 1, work (4 sc, ch 4, sl st in top of last sc made, 3 sc) in each corner ch-7 sp, work (3 sc, ch 4, sl st in top of last sc made, 2 sc) in each ch-5 sp across bottom, right and top edges; join left edge to right edge of adjacent panel as follows: work (3 sc, ch 2, sl st in corresponding ch-4 lp on adjacent panel, ch 2, sl st in top of last sc made, 2 sc) in each ch-5 sp across left edge: 215 ch-4 sps and 175 joined ch-4 sps; join with sl st in beg sc. Finish off; weave in ends.

Elegant Pineapples Tablecloth

The favorite classic motif of pineapples is used in squares in this tablecloth. Light and airy, it will be the perfect accent for a beautiful wood table.

SIZE: 48" x 84"

MATERIALS

Size 20 crochet thread
18 balls (400 yds each) or 7,200 yds natural
Tapestry needle
Stitch markers
Size 11 (1.1 mm) steel crochet hook
  (or size required for gauge)

GAUGE

Full motif = 12" x 12"
Rnds 1 and 2 = $1^1/2$" diameter
Rnds 1 through 9 = $5^1/2$" across center

SPECIAL STITCHES

Beginning shell (beg shell): Ch 4, (2 tr, ch 2, 3 tr) in same ch-2 sp as sl st or in specified st or sp: beg shell made.

Shell: (3 tr, ch 2, 3 tr) in next ch-2 sp or in specified st or sp: shell made.

5 triple decrease (5 tr dec): *YO twice, insert hook in next specified st or sp and draw up a lp, (YO and draw through 2 lps on hook) twice; rep from * 4 times more; YO and draw through all 6 lps on hook: 5 tr dec made.

7 tr decrease (7 tr dec): *YO twice, insert hook in next specified st or sp and draw up a lp, (YO and draw through 2 lps on hook) twice; rep from * 6 times more; YO and draw through all 8 lps on hook: 7 tr dec made.

Instructions

MOTIF

(make 28)

Ch 8; join with sl st to form a ring.

Rnd 1 (right side): Ch 4 (counts as tr), 2 tr in ring, ch 2; *3 tr in ring, ch 2; rep from * 6 times more: 24 tr and 8 ch-2 sps; join with sl st in 4th ch of beg ch-4.

Rnd 2: Sl st in next 2 tr and in next ch-2 sp, work beg shell; *shell, ch 3, shell; rep from * 3 times more omitting shell at end of last rep: 8 shells and 4 ch-3 sps; join as before.

Rnd 3: Sl st in next 2 tr and in next ch-2 sp, work beg shell; *ch 7, shell, ch 4, skip next ch-3 sp, shell; rep from * 3 times more omitting shell at end of last rep: 8 shells, 4 ch-7 sps and 4 ch-4 sps; join.

Rnd 4: Sl st in next 2 tr and in next ch-2 sp, work beg shell; *ch 3, 8 tr in 4th ch of ch-7 sp, ch 3, shell, ch 4, tr in next ch-4 sp, ch 4, shell; rep from * 3 times more omitting shell at end of last rep: 8 shells, 36 tr, 8 ch-3 sps and 8 ch-4 sps; join.

Rnd 5: Sl st in next 2 tr and in next ch-2 sp, work beg shell; *ch 5, skip next ch-3 sp, sc in next tr, (ch 6, sc in next tr) 7 times, ch 5, shell, (ch 4, tr in next ch-4 sp) 2 times, ch 4, shell; rep from * 3 times more omitting shell at end of last rep: 8 shells, 8 ch-5 sps, 12 ch-4 sps, 8 tr, 28 ch-6 sps and 32 sc; join.

Rnd 6: Sl st in next 2 tr and in next ch-2 sp, work beg shell; *ch 6, skip next ch-5 sp, (sc in next ch-6 sp, ch 6) 7 times, shell, (ch 4, tr in next ch-4 sp) 3 times, ch 4, shell; rep from * 3 times more omitting shell at end of last rep: 8 shells, 32 ch-6 sps, 28 sc, 12 tr and 16 ch-4 sps; join.

Rnd 7: Sl st in next 2 tr and in next ch-2 sp, work beg shell; *ch 6, skip next ch-6 sp, (sc in next ch-6 sp, ch 6) 6 times, shell, ch 4, tr in next ch-4 sp, ch 4, skip next ch-4 sp, 5 tr in next tr, ch 4, skip next ch-4 sp, tr in next ch-4 sp, ch 4, shell; rep from * 3 times more omitting shell at end of last rep: 8 shells, 28 ch-6 sps, 24 sc, 28 tr and 16 ch-4 sps; join.

Rnd 8: Sl st in next 2 tr and in next ch-2 sp, work beg shell; *ch 6, skip next ch-6 sp, (sc in next ch-6 sp, ch 6) 5 times, shell, (ch 4, tr in next ch-4 sp) 2 times, ch 4, 5 tr dec in next 5 tr, (ch 4, tr in next ch-4 sp) 2 times, ch 4, shell; rep from * 3 times more omitting shell at end of last rep: 8 shells, 24 ch-6 sps, 20 sc, 4 - 5 tr dec, 16 tr and 24 ch-4 sps; join.

Rnd 9: Sl st in next 2 tr and in next ch-2 sp, work beg shell; *ch 6, skip next ch-6 sp, (sc in next ch-6 sp, ch 6) 4 times, shell, (ch 4, tr in next ch-4 sp) 6 times, ch 4, shell; rep from * 3 times more omitting shell at end of last rep: 8 shells, 20 ch-6 sps, 16 sc, 24 tr and 28 ch-6 sps; join.

COMPLETE FIRST PINEAPPLE

Row 1: Sl st in next 2 tr and in next ch-2 sp; *work beg shell, ch 6, skip next ch-6 sp, (sc in next ch-6 sp, ch 6) 3 times, shell: 2 shells, 4 ch-6 sps and 3 sc; turn.

Row 2: Ch 4, shell, ch 6, skip next ch-6 sp, (sc in next ch-6 sp, ch 6) 2 times, shell: 2 shells, 3 ch-6 sps and 2 sc; turn.

Row 3: Ch 4, shell, ch 6, skip next ch-6 sp, sc in next ch-6 sp, ch 6, shell: 2 shells, 2 ch-6 sps and 1 sc; turn.

Row 4: Ch 4, shell, ch 6, sc in sc, ch 6, shell: 2 shells, 2 ch-6 sps and 1 sc; turn.

Row 5: Ch 4, shell, 3 tr in next ch-2 sp, remove lp from hook, insert hook in last ch-2 sp, draw lp through ch-2 sp, 3 tr in same ch-2 sp as last 3 tr: 1 shell and 6 tr. Finish off; weave in ends.

COMPLETE SECOND THROUGH FOURTH PINEAPPLES

Row 1: With right side facing, join thread with sl st in next ch-2 sp on Rnd 9, rep Row 1 on first pineapple from * to end.

Rows 2 through 5: Rep Rows 2 through 5 on first pineapple.

Rnd 10: With right side facing, join thread with sl st in beg ch-4 sp on Row 5 of any pineapple, work beg shell in same ch-4 sp as joining; *ch 9, shell around post of last tr on Row 5 of same pineapple, ch 4, tr in ch-4 sp at beg of Row 4, ch 4, tr around post of tr at end of Row 3, ch 4, tr in ch-4 sp at beg of Row 2, ch 4, tr around post of tr at end of Row 1, ch 4, tr in 5th tr of next shell on Rnd 9, (ch 4, tr in next ch-4 sp) 7 times, ch 4, tr in 2nd tr of next shell on Rnd 9, ch 4, tr in beg ch-4 sp on Row 1 of next pineapple, ch 4, tr

Motif

around post of tr at end of Row 2, ch 4, tr in beg
ch-4 sp on Row 3, ch 4, tr around post of tr at
end of Row 4, ch 4, shell in beg ch-4 sp on Row
5; rep from * 3 times more omitting shell at end
of last rep: 8 shells, 4 ch-9 sps, 68 tr and 72 ch-4
sps; join.

Rnd 11: Sl st in next 2 tr and in next ch-2 sp, work beg shell; **ch 3, 8 tr in 5th ch of ch-9 sp, ch 3, shell, (ch 4, tr in next ch-4 sp) 5 times; *ch 4, skip next ch-4 sp, 5 tr in next tr, skip next ch-4 sp, (ch 4, tr in next ch-4 sp) 4 times; rep from * once; ch 4, tr in next ch-4 sp, ch 4, shell; rep from ** 3 times more omitting shell at end of last rep: 8 shells, 8 ch-3 sps, 128 tr and 68 ch-4 sps; join.

Rnd 12: Sl st in next 2 tr and in next ch-2 sp, work beg shell; **ch 6, (sc in next tr, ch 6) 8 times, shell, (ch 4, tr in next ch-4 sp) 6 times; *ch 4, 5 tr dec in next 5 tr, (ch 4, tr in next ch-4 sp) 5 times; rep from * once; ch 4, tr in next ch-4 sp, ch 4, shell; rep from ** 3 times more omitting shell at end of last rep: 8 shells, 36 ch-6 sps, 32 sc, 8 - 5 tr dec, 68 tr and 80 ch-4 sps; join.

Rnd 13: Sl st in next 2 tr and in next ch-2 sp, work beg shell; *ch 6, skip next ch-6 sp, (sc in next ch-6 sp, ch 6) 7 times, shell, (ch 4, tr in next ch-4 sp) 20 times, ch 4, shell; rep from * 3 times more omitting shell at end of last rep: 8 shells, 32 ch-6 sps, 28 sc, 80 tr and 84 ch-4 sps; join.

Rnd 14: Sl st in next 2 tr and in next ch-2 sp, work beg shell; *ch 6, skip next ch-6 sp, (sc in next ch-6 sp, ch 6) 6 times, shell, (ch 4, tr in next ch-4 sp) 21 times, ch 4, shell; rep from * 3 times more omitting shell at end of last rep: 8 shells, 28 ch-6 sps, 24 sc, 84 tr and 88 ch-4 sps; join.

Rnd 15: Sl st in next 2 tr and in next ch-2 sp, work beg shell; ***ch 6, skip next ch-6 sp, (sc in next ch-6 sp, ch 6) 5 times, shell (place marker in this shell); *(ch 4, tr in next ch-4 sp) 2 times, ch 4, skip next ch-4 sp, 7 tr in next tr, skip next ch-4 sp, (ch 4, tr in next ch-4 sp) 2 times, ch 4**, skip next ch-4 sp, shell in next tr, skip next ch-4 sp; rep from * once; rep from * to ** once; shell; rep from *** 3 times more omitting shell at end of last rep: 16 shells, 24 ch-6 sps, 20 sc, 132 tr and 72 ch-4 sps; join.

Row 1: Sl st in next 2 tr and in next ch-2 sp; *work beg shell, ch 6, skip next ch-6 sp, (sc in next ch-6 sp, ch 6) 4 times, shell: 2 shells, 5 ch-6 sps and 4 sc; turn.

Row 2: Ch 4, shell, ch 6, skip next ch-6 sp, (sc in next ch-6 sp, ch 6) 3 times, shell: 2 shells, 4 ch-6 sps and 3 sc; turn.

Row 3: Ch 4, shell, ch 6, skip next ch-6 sp, (sc in next ch-6 sp, ch 6) 2 times, shell: 2 shells, 3 ch-6 sps and 2 sc; turn.

Row 4: Ch 4, shell, ch 6, skip next ch-6 sp, sc in next ch-6 sp, ch 6, shell: 2 shells, 2 ch-6 sps and 1 sc; turn.

Row 5: Ch 4, shell, ch 6, sc in sc, ch 6, shell: 2 shells, 2 ch-6 sps and 1 sc; turn.

Row 6: Ch 4, shell, ch 1, shell: 2 shells and 1 ch-1 sp; turn.

Row 7: Ch 1, sc in first 3 tr and in next ch-2 sp, shell in ch between shells, sc in next ch-2 sp and in next 3 tr: 1 shell and 8 sc. Finish off, leaving a 12" end for joining.

Row 1: With right side facing, skip next 2 shells on Rnd 15, join thread with sl st in ch-2 sp of shell before next pineapple, rep Row 1 on first pineapple from * to end.

Rows 2 through 7: Rep Rows 2 through 7 on first pineapple.

FIRST SIDE

Row 1: With right side facing, join thread with sl st in 5th tr of any marked shell on Rnd 15, work beg shell in same tr as joining; *skip next ch-4 sp, (ch 4, tr in next ch-4 sp) 2 times, ch 4, 7 tr dec in next 7 tr, (ch 4, tr in next ch-4 sp) 2 times, ch 4**, 3 tr in 2nd tr of next shell, ch 2 (place marker in this ch-2 sp), 3 tr in ch-2 sp of same shell, ch 2, 3 tr in 5th tr of same shell; rep from * once; rep from * to ** once; shell in 2nd tr of next shell: 2 shells, 3 - 7 tr dec, 30 tr, 4 ch-2 sps and 18 ch-4 sps; turn.

FIRST SIDE POINT

Row 1: Ch 4, shell; *skip next ch-4 sp, ch 4, tr in next ch-4 sp, ch 4*, tr in 7 tr dec; rep from * to * once; shell: 2 shells, 4 ch-4 sps and 3 tr; turn.

Row 2: Ch 4, shell, skip next ch-4 sp, (ch 4, tr in next ch-4 sp) 2 times, ch 4, shell: 2 shells, 3 ch-4 sps and 2 tr; turn.

Row 3: Ch 4, shell, skip next ch-4 sp, sc in next ch-4 sp, shell: 2 shells and 1 sc; turn.

Row 4: Ch 1, sc in first 3 tr and in next ch-2 sp, shell in sc, sc in next ch-2 sp and in next 3 tr: 1 shell and 8 sc. Finish off, leaving a 12" end for joining.

SECOND SIDE POINT

Row 1: With wrong side facing, join thread with sl st in 2nd marked ch-2 sp on Row 1 of same side, work beg shell; *skip next ch-4 sp, ch 4, tr in next ch-4 sp, ch 4*, tr in 7 tr dec; rep from * to * once; shell in next ch-2 sp: 2 shells, 4 ch-4 sps and 3 tr; turn.

Rows 2 through 4: Rep Rows 2 through 4 on first side point.

THIRD SIDE POINT

Row 1: With wrong side facing, join thread with sl st in first marked ch-2 sp on Row 1 of same side, work beg shell; *skip next ch-4 sp, ch 4, tr in next ch-4 sp, ch 4*, tr in 7th tr dec; rep from * to * once; shell: 2 shells, 4 ch-4 sps and 3 tr; turn.

Rows 2 through 4: Rep Rows 2 through 4 on first side point.

Second through Fourth Sides

Rep first side and 3 side points on remaining 3 sides of motif.

JOINING

Hold 2 motifs with right sides tog. With tapestry needle and thread, with overcast st sew motifs tog through both lps of 8 sts on Row 7 of 2 corner pineapples and through both lps of 16 sts on Row 4 of 3 side points between 2 joined corner pineapples. Join into 4 rows of 7 motifs each.

Peacock Filet Bedspread

Designed by Ann Orr

Ann Orr was one of the most popular and talented needlework designers in America in the early part of the 20th century. Between 1914 and 1945 in addition to raising three daughters, she published hundreds of design leaflets and served as the editor of two women's magazines including Good Housekeeping, where she served as the needlework editor for over 20 years. She was so beloved that well into the 1970s she continued to receive mail addressed to her at the magazine.

One of her favorite design techniques was the block-by-block design of charts. She intended these designs to be used not only for filet crochet but for needlepoint, cross stitch and even quiltmaking.

This peacock filet bedspread is one of her most famous designs and will add a dramatic touch to any bedroom. The central peacock is framed by rows of lacet stitch, and bordered with charming basket motifs.

For another filet piece probably designed by Ann Orr, see page 120.

SIZE: 78" x 68" plus fringe

MATERIALS
Size 20 crochet cotton,
   34 balls (400 yds each) or 13,600 yds ecru
Size 10 (1.30 mm) steel crochet hook
   (or size required for gauge)

GAUGE
17 mesh = 4 1/8"; 17 mesh rows = 4"

Instructions

CENTER SECTION

Ch 804.

Row 1 (right side): Starting on Row 37 on Bottom Right and Bottom Left charts, dc in 9th ch from hook (beg open mesh made); *ch 2, skip next 2 chs, dc in next ch (open mesh made)*; rep from * to * 3 times more; dc in next 9 chs (3 closed mesh made); rep from * to * 5 times more; dc in next 6 chs (2 closed mesh made); rep from * to * 21 times more; dc in next 3 chs (1 closed mesh made); rep from * to * 192 times more; dc in next 3 chs (1 closed mesh made), rep from * to * 21 times more; dc in next 6 chs (2 closed mesh made); rep from * to * 5 times more; dc in next 9 chs (3 closed mesh made); rep from * to * 5 times more: 12 closed mesh and 254 open mesh; ch 5, turn.

Work open mesh, closed mesh and lacets as per Bottom Right, Bottom Left, Top Right and Top Left charts and filet instructions on pages 134-138 from Row 38 to top of Top Right and Top Left charts. At end of last row, finish off; weave in

ends. Turn piece upside down so foundation ch is at top and wrong side is facing. Join with sl st in 6th skipped ch at beg of Row 1 (Row 37 on Bottom Right and Bottom Left charts). Turn Bottom Right and Bottom Left charts upside down and work bottom 36 rows as per charts and filet instructions.

Note: *Last 6 rows along top and bottom are worked one section at a time. Each section is joined and finished off to create contoured edges.*

EDGINGS

Right Edging

Row 1 (right side): With right side facing and working across edge of rows, join with sl st in top of last dc at bottom right-hand corner of Center Section, ch 5, dc in 3rd ch of turning ch-5 on next row (beg open mesh made); *ch 2, dc in top of dc or in 3rd ch of turning ch-5 on next row (open mesh made)*; rep from * to * across right edge to foundation ch; ch 2, dc in 6th skipped ch at beg of Row 1 (Row 37 on Bottom Right and Bottom Left charts); rep from * to * across right edge, ending with dc in 3rd ch of turning ch-5 at top right-hand corner: 331 open mesh; ch 3 (counts as dc on next row now and through-out), turn.

Row 2: (Work 2 dc in next ch-2 sp, dc in next dc) 3 times (3 closed mesh made); *ch 2, skip next 2 chs, sc in next dc, ch 2, skip next 2 chs, dc in next dc (partial lacet made); rep from * across to last 2 open mesh; 2 dc in next ch-2 sp, dc in next dc (1 closed mesh made); 2 dc in beg ch-5 sp, dc in 3rd ch of beg ch-5 (1 closed mesh made): 5 closed mesh and 163 partial lacets; ch 3, turn.

Row 3: Dc in next 6 dc; *ch 5, skip next sc, dc in next dc (partial lacet made); rep from * across to last 9 dc; dc in last 9 dc (including 3rd ch of turning ch-3): 5 closed mesh and 163 partial lacets; ch 3, turn.

Row 4: Dc in next 9 dc; *ch 2, skip next 2 chs, sc in next ch, ch 2, skip next 2 chs, dc in next dc (partial lacet made); rep from * across to last 6 dc;

dc in last 6 dc: 5 closed mesh and 163 partial lacets; ch 3, turn.

Rows 5 through 11: Rep Rows 3 and 4 three times more, then rep Row 3 once more.

Row 12: Dc in next 9 dc; *ch 2, skip next 2 chs, dc in next ch, ch 2, skip next 2 chs, dc in next dc; rep from * across to last 6 dc; dc in last 6 dc: 5 closed mesh and 326 open mesh. Finish off; weave in ends.

Left Edging

Row 1 (right side): With right side facing and working across edge of rows, join with sl st in top of last dc at top left-hand corner of Center Section, ch 5, dc in 3rd ch of turning ch-5 on next row (beg open mesh made); *ch 2, dc in top of dc or in 3rd ch of turning ch-5 on next row (open mesh made)*; rep from * to * across left edge to foundation ch; ch 2, dc in first ch of foundation ch at end of Row 1 (Row 37 on Bottom Right and Bottom Left charts); rep from * to * across left edge, ending with dc in 3rd ch of turning ch-5 at bottom left-hand corner: 331 open mesh; ch 3 (counts as dc on next row now and throughout), turn.

Rows 2 through 12: Rep Rows 2 through 12 on Right Edging.

CORNERS

Top Right-Hand Corner

Row 1: With right side facing, join with sl st in top of last dc on Row 3 of Edging at top right-hand corner; ch 3, 2 dc around post of same dc, dc in 3rd ch of turning ch-3 on Row 2 of Edging, 2 dc in turning ch-3 sp, dc in top of last dc on Row 1 of Edging, 2 dc around post of same dc; working across top row at corner of Center Section, dc in last dc or in 3rd ch of turning ch-5 (at base of last dc on Row 1 of Edging), 2 dc in next ch-2 sp or in turning ch-5 sp, dc in next dc; (ch 2, skip next 2 chs, dc in next dc) 4 times; (2 dc in next ch-2 sp, dc in next dc) 2 times; dc in next 6 dc: 8 closed mesh and 4 open mesh; turn.

Rows 2 through 6: Work open mesh and closed mesh as per Corners chart and filet instructions on pages 134-138.

Bottom Left-Hand Corner

Rows 1 through 6: Work same as Rows 1 through 6 on Top Right-Hand Corner, joining with sl st in top of last dc on Row 3 of Edging at bottom left-hand corner.

Top Left-Hand Corner

Row 1: With wrong side facing, join with sl st in 3rd ch of turning ch-3 on Row 3 of Edging at top left-hand corner; ch 3, 2 dc in turning ch-3 sp, dc in top of last dc on Row 2 of Edging, 2 dc around post of same dc, dc in 3rd ch of beg ch-5 on Row 1 of Edging, 2 dc in beg ch-5 sp; working across top row at corner of Center Section, dc in last dc or in 3rd ch of turning ch-5 (at base of beg ch-5 on Row 1 of Edging), 2 dc in next ch-2 sp or in turning ch-5 sp, dc in next dc; (ch 2, skip next 2 chs, dc in next dc) 4 times; (2 dc in next ch-2 sp, dc in next dc) 2 times; dc in next 6 dc: 8 closed mesh and 4 open mesh; turn.

Rows 2 through 6: Work open mesh and closed mesh as per Corners chart and filet instructions on pages 134-138.

Bottom Right-Hand Corner

Rows 1 through 6: Work same as Rows 1 through 6 on Top Left-Hand Corner, joining with sl st in 3rd ch of turning ch-3 on Row 3 of Edging at bottom right-hand corner.

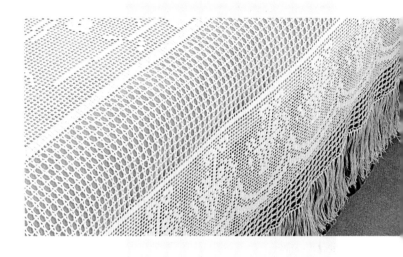

FRINGE

Following Fringe Instructions on page 142, cut 10" long strands of thread. Knot 4 strands in each ch-2 sp on Row 12 of Right and Left Edgings: 326 fringes on Right Edging and 326 fringes on Left Edging.

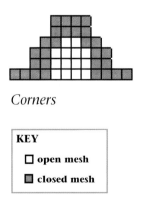

Corners

KEY
☐ open mesh
■ closed mesh

—160
—150
—140
—130
—120
—110
—100
—90
—80
—70
—60
—50
—40
—37
—30
—20
—10

KEY

☐ open mesh

■ closed mesh

▨ lacets

Bottom Left

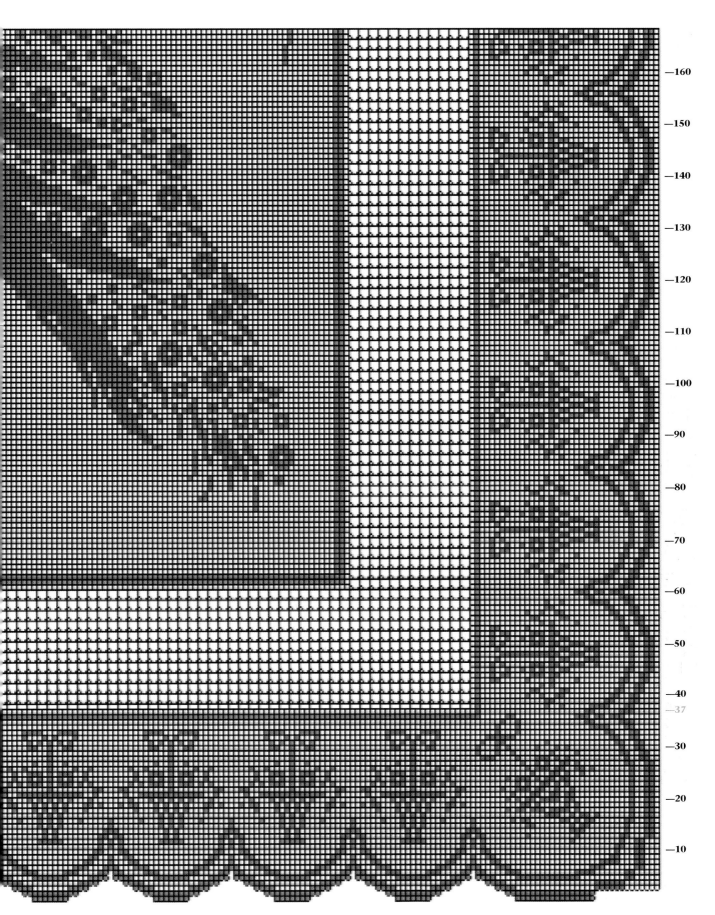

Bottom Right

—160

—150

—140

—130

—120

—110

—100

—90

—80

—70

—60

—50

—40

—37

—30

—20

—10

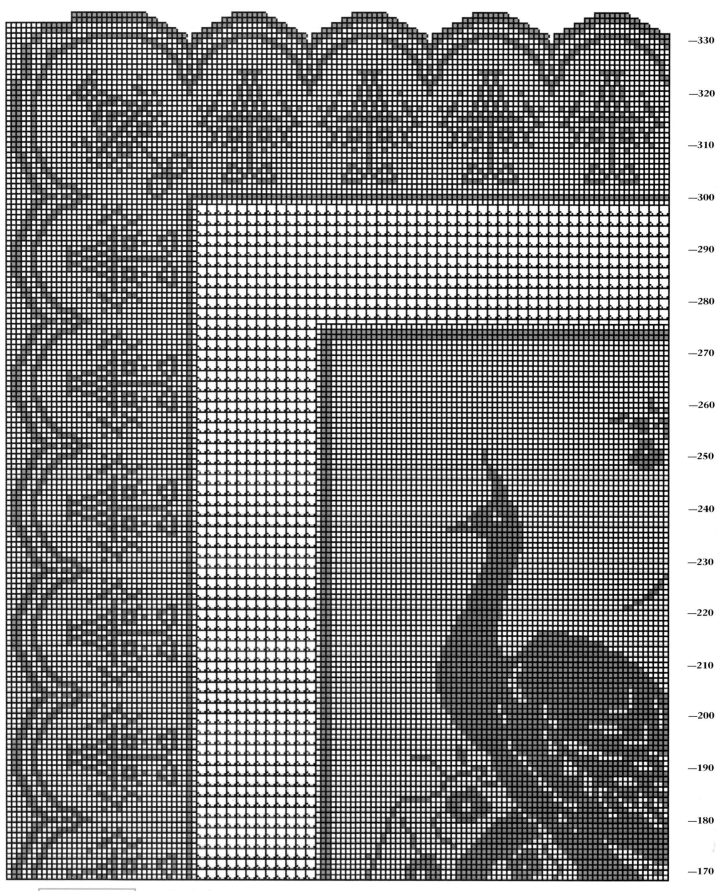

—330
—320
—310
—300
—290
—280
—270
—260
—250
—240
—230
—220
—210
—200
—190
—180
—170

Top Left

KEY
☐ open mesh
▨ closed mesh
◹ lacets

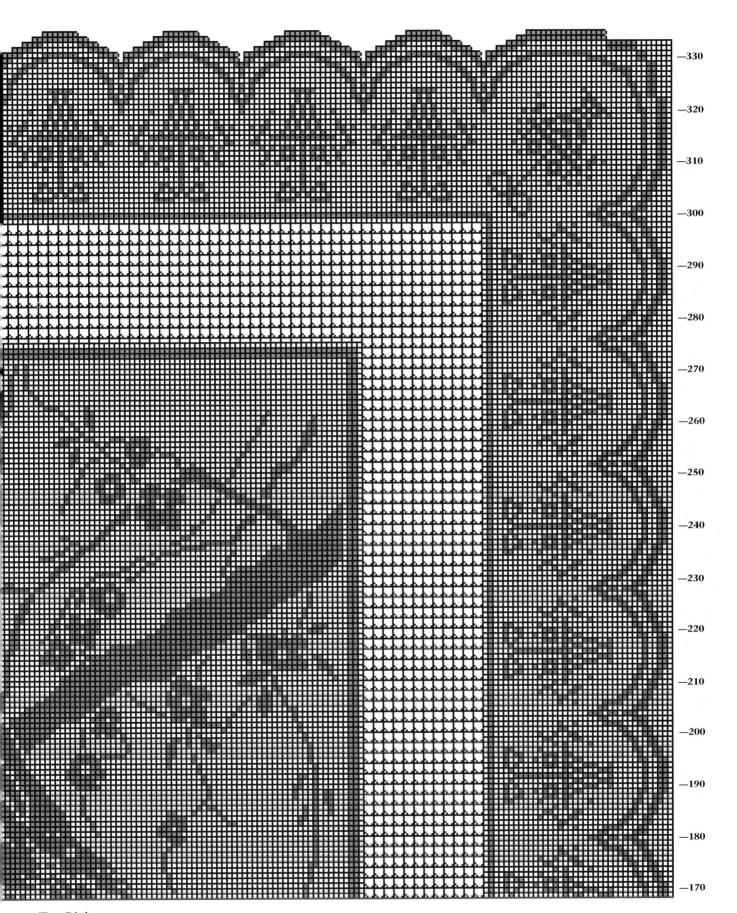

—330
—320
—310
—300
—290
—280
—270
—260
—250
—240
—230
—220
—210
—200
—190
—180
—170

Top Right

35

Pineapple Ovals Tablecloth

An unusual oval motif featuring pineapples forms the design for this cloth. Square joining motifs add an elegant touch.

SIZE: 58" wide x 80" long

MATERIALS

Size 20 crochet thread
17 balls (400 yds each) or 6,800 yds ecru
Size 9 (1.40 mm) steel crochet hook
    (or size required for gauge)
stitch markers

GAUGE

Motif A = 6 1/2" x 3 1/2"

Motif B = 3 1/4" square and 4 1/2" diagonally between points

SPECIAL STITCHES

3 dc decrease (3 dc dec): *YO, insert hook in specified st and draw up a lp, YO and draw through 2 lps on hook; rep from * 2 times more; YO and draw through all 4 lps on hook: 3 dc dec made.

4 dc decrease (4 dc dec): *YO, insert hook in specified st and draw up a lp, YO and draw through 2 lps on hook; rep from * 3 times more; YO and draw through all 5 lps on hook: 4 dc dec made.

Instructions

MOTIF A (MARQUISE SHAPE)

First Motif

Ch 5, join with sl st to form a ring.

Rnd 1 (right side): Ch 4 (counts as dc and ch-1 sp); (dc, ch 1) 11 times in ring: 12 dc and 12 ch-1 sps; join with sl st in 3rd ch of beg ch-4.

Rnd 2: Ch 3 (counts as dc now and throughout), 2 dc in same ch as joining; *ch 3, skip next dc, dc in next ch-1 sp, ch 3, skip next dc**; 3 dc in next dc; rep from * 2 times more; rep from * to ** once: 16 dc and 8 ch-3 sps; join in 3rd ch of beg ch-3.

Rnd 3: Ch 3, dc in same ch as joining; *ch 1, skip next dc, 2 dc in next dc, ch 3, (dc, ch 3, dc) in next dc, ch 3**; 2 dc in next dc; rep from * 2 times more; rep from * to ** once: 24 dc, 12 ch-3 sps and 4 ch-1 sps; join as before.

Rnd 4: Ch 3, dc in next dc; *ch 3, dc in next 2 dc, ch 3, skip next ch-3 sp, 5 dc in next ch-3 sp, ch 3, skip next ch-3 sp, (dc in next 2 dc, ch 3) 2 times; skip next ch-3 sp, 7 tr in next ch-3 sp, ch 3, skip next ch-3 sp**; dc in next 2 dc; rep from * to ** once: 14 tr, 26 dc and 12 ch-3 sps; join.

Rnd 5: Ch 3, dc in next dc; *ch 1, dc in next 2 dc, ch 4, (dc in next dc, ch 1) 4 times, dc in next dc, ch 4, dc in next 2 dc, ch 1, dc in next 2 dc, ch 5, (tr in next tr, ch 1) 6 times, tr in next tr, ch 5**; dc in next 2 dc; rep from * to ** once: 14 tr, 26 dc, 4 ch-5 sps, 4 ch-4 sps and 24 ch-1 sps; join.

Motif A

Rnd 6: Ch 3, dc in next dc; *skip next ch, dc in next 2 dc, ch 5, (dc in next dc, ch 3, sc in next dc, ch 3) 2 times, dc in next dc, ch 5, dc in next 2 dc, skip next ch, dc in next 2 dc, ch 5, 3 dc in 3rd ch of next ch-5, (ch 3, sc in next ch-1 sp) 6 times, ch 3, 3 dc in 3rd ch of next ch-5, ch 5**; dc in next 2 dc; rep from * to ** once: 34 dc, 16 sc, 8 ch-5 sps and 22 ch-3 sps; join.

Rnd 7: Ch 2, 3 dc dec in next 3 dc; *ch 7, sc in next ch-5 sp, ch 7, skip next dc, sc in next dc, ch 7, skip next dc, sc in next ch-5 sp, ch 7, 4 dc dec in next 4 dc, ch 7, sc in next ch-5 sp, ch 7, skip next 2 dc, 3 dc in next dc, ch 3, skip next ch-3 sp, (sc in next ch-3 sp, ch 3) 5 times, 3 dc in next dc, ch 7, sc in next ch-5 sp**; ch 7, 4 dc dec in next 4 dc; rep from * to ** once; ch 3, tr in top of 3 dc dec to form last ch-7 sp: one 3 dc dec, three 4 dc dec, 12 dc, 20 sc, 16 ch-7 sps and 12 ch-3 sps.

Rnd 8: (Ch 5, sc in next ch-7 sp) 2 times; *ch 5, sc in next sc, (ch 5, sc in next ch-7 sp) 4 times, ch 5, skip next 2 dc, 3 dc in next dc, ch 3, skip next ch-3 sp, (sc in next ch-3 sp, ch 3) 4 times, 3 dc in next dc**; (ch 5, sc in next ch-7 sp) 4 times, place marker in 2nd ch-5 sp just made; rep from * to ** once, omitting marker; ch 5, sc in next ch-7 sp, ch 1, tr in joining tr to form last ch-5 sp: 12 dc, 25 sc, 20 ch-5 sps and 10 ch-3 sps; ch 5, turn, leaving rem sts unworked.

Row 1 (wrong side): Sc in next ch-5 sp, ch 5, skip next 2 dc, 3 dc in next dc, ch 3, skip next ch-3 sp, (sc in next ch-3 sp, ch 3) 3 times, 3 dc in next dc, ch 5, sc in next ch-5 sp; ch 1, tr in next ch-5 sp to form last ch-5 sp: 6 dc, 3 sc, 4 ch-5 sps and 4 ch-3 sps; ch 5, turn.

Row 2 (right side): Sc in next ch-5 sp, ch 5, skip next 2 dc, 3 dc in next dc, ch 3, skip next ch-3 sp, (sc in next ch-3 sp, ch 3) 2 times, 3 dc in next dc, ch 5, sc in next ch-5 sp; ch 1, tr in next ch-5 sp: 6 dc, 2 sc, 4 ch-5 sps and 3 ch-3 sps; ch 5, turn.

Row 3: Sc in next ch-5 sp, ch 5, skip next 2 dc, 3 dc in next dc, ch 3, skip next ch-3 sp, sc in next ch-3 sp, ch 3, 3 dc in next dc, ch 5, sc in next ch-5 sp; ch 1, tr in next ch-5 sp: 6 dc, 1 sc, 4 ch-5 sps and 2 ch-3 sps; ch 5, turn.

Row 4: Sc in next ch-5 sp, ch 5, skip next 2 dc, 3 dc in next dc, skip next 2 ch-3 sps, 3 dc in next dc, ch 5, sc in next ch-5 sp; ch 1, tr in next ch-5 sp: 6 dc and 4 ch-5 sps; ch 5, turn.

Row 5: Sc in next ch-5 sp, ch 5, skip next 2 dc, dc in next 2 dc, ch 5, sc in next ch-5 sp; ch 1, tr in next ch-5 sp: 2 dc, 2 sc and 4 ch-5 sps; ch 5, turn.

38

Row 6: Dc in next 2 ch-5 sps; ch 1, tr in next ch-5 sp: 2 dc and 2 ch-5 sps; ch 5, turn.

Row 7: Sl st in next ch-5 sp, place marker in ch-5 sp just made: 1 sl st and 1 ch-5 sp. Finish off; weave in ends.

SECOND PINEAPPLE TIP

With wrong side facing, join with sl st in marked ch-5 sp on Rnd 8, ch 5.

Rows 1 through 6: Rep Rows 1 through 6 on First Pineapple Tip.

Row 7: Sc in next ch-5 sp: 1 sc and 1 ch-5 sp; ch 1, turn.

EDGING

Work (2 sc, ch 5, 2 sc) in next ch-5 sp (tip of motif made); *(2 sc, ch 3, 2 sc) in next ch-5 sp*; rep from * to * around to marked ch-5 sp on Row 7 of First Pineapple Tip; (2 sc, ch 5, 2 sc) in marked ch-5 sp (tip of motif made); rep from * to * around to beg: 168 sc, 2 ch-5 sps and 40 ch-3 sps; join with sl st in first sc. Finish off; weave in ends.

Note: *Join all motifs with wrong sides together.*

JOINED MOTIF A

Work Joined Motif A same as First Motif A through Row 7 of Second Pineapple Tip.

Note: *Edging of Motif A is joined to edging of adjacent Motif A in ch-5 sp at tip of motif and in next three ch-3 sps before or after joined ch-5 sp at tip of motif. Begin by joining four Motif A into a circle (see* **Fig. 1**). *Join two more Motif A to first circle (see shaded part of* **Fig. 2**). *Join two more Motif A to joined motif to form second joined circle (see shaded part of* **Fig. 3**).*

1

2

3

Join Motif A into rows of joined circles in same manner as follows: Make three rows of 8 joined circles for center of tablecloth (see **Fig. 4**), *joining Motif A to previous row as you make new row.*

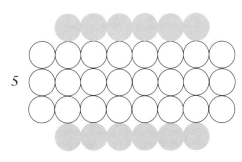

4

Join Motif A to form a row of 6 joined circles centered on each long edge of rows of 8 joined circles (see shaded part of **Fig 5**), *joining Motif A to previous row as you make new row.*

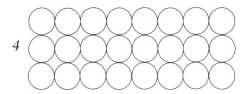

5

Join Motif A to form a row of 5 joined half circles centered on each long edge of rows of 6 joined circles (see shaded parts of **Fig 6**), *joining Motif A to previous row as you make new row. Join one Motif A diagonally between rows of 6 joined circles and rows of 8 joined circles at ends of rows (see shaded parts of* **Fig 6**).*

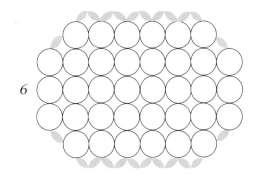

6

Motif B

EDGING

Work joined and unjoined ch sps around Motif A
as follows: work (2 sc, ch 5, 2 sc) in unjoined ch-5
sp at end of Motif A as needed; work (2 sc, ch 3,
2 sc) in each unjoined ch-3 sp of Motif A as needed; to join ch-5 sp at tip of Motif A, work 2 sc in
ch-5 sp of current Motif A, ch 2, sc in ch-5 sp at
tip of adjacent Motif A, ch 2, 2 sc in same ch-5 sp
of current Motif A; to join ch-3 sp of Motif A,
work 2 sc in ch-3 sp of current Motif A, ch 1, sc in
corresponding ch-3 sp of adjacent Motif A, ch 1,
sc in same ch-3 sp on current Motif A: 168 sc on
current motif, 2 joined or unjoined ch-5 sps and
40 joined or unjoined ch-3 sps; join with sl st in
first sc. Finish off; weave in ends.

MOTIF B (CENTER JOINING MOTIF)

Note: Join Motif B in the center of each 4 Motif A
throughout tablecloth (see photograph).

Ch 5, join with sl st to form a ring.

Rnd 1 (right side): Ch 7 (counts as tr and ch-3
sp); *tr in ring, ch 3; rep from * 6 times more:
8 tr and 8 ch-3 sps; join with sl st in 4th ch of beg
ch-7.

Rnd 2: Ch 1, sc in same ch as joining; *5 sc in
next ch-3 sp, sc in next tr; rep from * 6 times
more; 5 sc in next ch-3 sp: 48 sc; join with sl st in
first sc.

Rnd 3: Ch 9 (counts as tr and ch-5 sp); *skip 2 sc,
sc in next sc, ch 5, skip 2 sc**; tr in next sc, ch 5;
rep from * 6 times more; rep from * to ** once: 8
tr, 8 sc and 16 ch-5 sps; join with sl st in 4th ch of
beg ch-9.

Rnd 4: Ch 1, sc in same ch as joining, ch 10; *sc
in next tr, ch 10; rep from * 6 times more: 8 sc
and 8 ch-10 sps; join with sl st in first sc.

Rnd 5: Sl st in next ch-10 sp, ch 4 (counts as tr),
4 tr in same ch sp; *ch 11, dc in 6th ch from
hook, (ch 1, skip next ch, dc in next ch) 2 times;
ch 1, skip next ch, dc in top of last tr made; 5 tr
in same ch sp as last tr made; 14 tr in next ch-10
sp**; 5 tr in next ch-10 sp; rep from * 2 times
more; rep from * to ** once: 96 tr, 16 dc and 28
ch sps; join with sl st in 4th ch of beg ch-4.

Rnd 6 (joining): Ch 1, sc in same ch as joining, sc
in next 4 tr; *sc in next ch sp, ch 5, sc in 8th ch-3
sp after ch-5 sp at tip of adjacent Motif A, ch 5, sc
in same ch sp on current motif; 2 sc in each of
next 2 ch sps; sc in next ch sp, ch 5, sc in 6th ch-
3 sp after ch-5 sp at tip of same adjacent Motif A,
ch 5, (sc, ch 3, sc) in same ch sp on current motif;
ch 5, sc in 6th ch-3 sp before ch-5 sp at tip of
next adjacent Motif A, ch 5, sc in same ch sp on
current motif; 2 sc in each of next 2 ch sps; sc in
next ch sp, ch 5, sc in 8th ch-3 sp before ch-5 sp
at tip of same adjacent Motif A, ch 5, sc in same

ch sp on current motif; skip next dc, sc in next 10 tr; ch 2, sc in 10th ch-3 sp before ch-5 sp at tip of same adjacent Motif A, ch 2, sc in next 4 tr on current motif; ch 2, sc in 10th ch-3 sp after ch-5 sp at other tip of same adjacent Motif A (next ch-3 sp on same adjacent Motif A), ch 2**; sc in next 10 tr on current motif; rep from * 2 times more; rep from * to ** once; sc in next 5 tr on current motif: 160 sc and 24 joining ch lps; join with sl st in first sc. Finish off; weave in ends.

Filet Flower Baskets Bedroom Set

Dramatic stylized flower baskets are the theme for this beautiful bedspread and matching pillow toppers. Baskets, which were a favorite theme of crochet designers during the early part of the twentieth century, remain a favorite today.

BEDSPREAD SIZE: 71" x 79"

PILLOW TOPPER SIZE: 28$1/2$" x 13$1/2$"

MATERIALS

Size 10 (bedspread weight) crochet thread
    24 balls (400 yds each) or 9,600 yds cream (for bedspread)
    2 $1/2$ balls (400 yds each) or 1,000 yds cream (for pillow toppers)
    7 balls (400 yds each) or 2,800 yds lt green (for bedspread)
    $1/2$ ball (400 yds each) or 200 yds lt green (for pillow toppers)
Size 8 (1.50 mm) steel crochet hook
    (or size required for gauge)

GAUGE

17 mesh = 5"; 19$1/2$ rows = 5"
Square with border (on bedspread) =
    11$1/2$" wide x 11" high
Square (on pillow toppers) =
    10$1/2$" wide x 10$1/2$" high

Instructions

BEDSPREAD

Square (make 42)

With cream, ch 111.

Row 1 (right side): Dc in 9th ch from hook (skipped chs count as dc and ch-2 sp); *ch 2, skip 2 chs, dc in next ch; rep from * across: 36 dc and 35 ch-2 sps; ch 5 (counts as dc and ch-2 sp on next row now and throughout), turn.

Row 2: Dc in next dc; *ch 2, skip next 2 chs, dc in next dc; rep from * across: 36 dc and 35 ch-2 sps; ch 5, turn.

Rows 3 through 39: Work open and closed filet mesh as per chart and filet instructions on pages 134-138. At end of Row 39, finish off; weave in ends.

BORDER

Rnd 1: With right side facing, join lt green with sl st in 2nd dc worked on Row 39, ch 5, skip next 2 chs, dc in next dc; *ch 2, skip next 2 chs, dc in next dc; rep from * 29 times more; 2 dc in next ch-2 sp, dc in next dc, 7 dc in next corner sp, dc in ch at base of next dc, 2 dc in next ch sp on left edge of square, dc in top of next dc; ch 2, dc in ch at base of same dc; **ch 2, dc in top of next dc, ch 2, dc in ch at base of same dc; rep from ** 16 times more; 2 dc in next ch sp, dc in top of next dc, 7 dc in next corner sp, dc in ch at base of next dc on bottom edge, 2 dc in next ch sp, dc in ch at base of next dc; ***ch 2, skip next 2 chs, dc in ch at base of next dc; rep from *** 30

times more; 2 dc in next ch sp, dc in ch at base of next dc, 7 dc in next corner sp; dc in ch at base of next dc on right edge of square, 2 dc around post of same dc, dc in top of same dc; ****ch 2, dc in ch at base of next dc, ch 2, dc in top of same dc; rep from **** 16 times more; ch 2, dc in ch at base of next dc, 2 dc around post of same dc, dc in top of same dc, 7 dc in next corner sp, dc in next dc on top edge, 2 dc in next ch-2 sp; join with sl st in 3rd ch of beg ch-5.

Rnd 2: Ch 5, skip next 2 chs, dc in next dc; *ch 2, skip next 2 chs, dc in next dc*; rep from * to * 29 times more; **dc in next 5 dc, 2 dc in each of next 3 dc, dc in next 6 dc**; rep from * to * 35 times more; rep from ** to ** once; rep from * to * 31 times more; rep from ** to ** once; rep from * to * 35 times more; dc in next 5 dc, 2 dc in each of next 3 dc, dc in next 5 dc; join with sl st in 3rd ch of beg ch-5. Finish off; weave in ends.

JOINING

With right sides facing, whip stitch squares together with lt green into 7 rows with 6 squares in each row, leaving center 4 dc in each corner unjoined.

EDGING

Rnd 1: With right side facing, join cream with sl st in last dc of top left corner dc group, ch 3, 2 dc in same dc as joining, ch 6; in each section of dc and ch-2 sps between corner dc groups along left and right edges work: *skip next dc, 3 dc in next dc, ch 6**; rep from * to ** 16 times more; in each joined corner dc group work: 3 dc in 2nd dc of corner dc group, ch 6; ***skip next 3 dc, 3 dc in next dc, ch 6****; skip rem unjoined dc of corner dc group on current square and next 2 unjoined dc of corner dc group on next square, 3 dc in next dc, ch 6; rep from *** to **** 2 times more; in each of 4 corner dc group work: 3 dc in 2nd dc of corner dc group, ch 6; rep from *** to **** 4 times more; in each section of dc and ch-2 sps between corner dc groups along top and

bottom edges work: rep from * to ** 15 times more; on final corner dc group, omit final rep; join with sl st in 3rd ch of beg ch-3.

Rnd 2: Ch 3, dc in next 2 dc, ch 6; *dc in next 3 dc, ch 6; rep from * around; join with sl st in 3rd ch of beg ch-3. Finish off; weave in ends.

Rnd 3: With right side facing, join lt green with sl st in same ch as joining; ch 3, dc in next 2 dc, ch 3, sc in next ch-6 sp, ch 3; *dc in next 3 dc, ch 3, sc in next ch-6 sp, ch 3; rep from * around; join with sl st in 3rd ch of beg ch-3. Finish off; weave in ends.

Square (make 4)

With cream, ch 111.

Row 1 (right side): Dc in 9th ch from hook (skipped chs count as dc and ch-2 sp); *ch 2, skip 2 chs, dc in next ch; rep from * across: 36 dc and 35 ch-2 sps; ch 5 (counts as dc and ch-2 sp on next row now and throughout), turn.

Row 2: Dc in next dc; *ch 2, skip next 2 chs, dc in next dc; rep from * across: 36 dc and 35 ch-2 sps; ch 5, turn.

Rows 3 through 41: Work open and closed filet mesh as per chart and filet instructions on pages 134-138. At end of Row 41, finish off; weave in ends.

Center Panel (make 2)

With cream, ch 57.

Row 1 (right side): Dc in 9th ch from hook (skipped chs count as dc and ch-2 sp; *ch 2, skip 2 chs, dc in next ch; rep from * across: 18 dc and 17 ch-2 sps; ch 5 (counts as dc and ch-2 sp on next row now and throughout), turn.

Row 2: Dc in next dc; *ch 2, skip next 2 chs, dc in next dc; rep from * across: 18 dc and 17 ch-2 sps; ch 5, turn.

Rows 3 through 41: Work open and closed filet mesh as per chart and filet instructions on pages 134-138. At end of Row 41, finish off; weave in ends.

JOINING

With right sides facing, whip stitch center panel between two squares with cream. Repeat for second pillow topper.

BORDER

Rnd 1: With right side facing, join lt green with sl st in 2nd dc worked on Row 41 of square on right of center panel, ch 5, skip next 2 chs, dc in next dc; *ch 2, skip next 2 chs, dc in next dc*; rep from * to * 30 times more across top of right

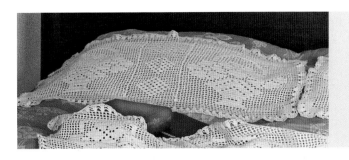

square; ch 2, skip next 2 chs, dc in joining of right square and center panel; rep from * to * 16 times more across top of center panel; ch 2, skip next 2 chs, dc in joining of center panel and left square; rep from * to * 33 times more across top of left square; 2 dc in next ch-2 sp, dc in next dc, 7 dc in next corner sp, dc in ch at base of next dc, 2 dc in next ch sp on left edge of left square, dc in top of next dc; ch 2, dc in ch at base of same dc; **ch 2, dc in top of next dc, ch 2, dc in ch at base of same dc; rep from ** 17 times more; 2 dc in next ch sp, dc in top of next dc, 7 dc in next corner sp, dc in ch at base of next dc on bottom edge of left square, 2 dc in next ch sp, dc in ch at base of next dc; ***ch 2, skip next 2 chs, dc in ch at base of next dc***; rep from *** to *** 31 times more across bottom of left square; ch 2, skip next 2 chs, dc in joining of left square and center panel; rep from *** to *** 16 times more across bottom of center panel; ch 2, skip next 2 chs, dc in joining of center panel and right square; rep from *** to *** 33 times more across bottom of right square; 2 dc in next ch-2 sp, dc in ch at base of next dc, 7 dc in next corner sp; dc in ch at base of next dc on right edge of right square, 2 dc around post of same dc, dc in top of same dc; ****ch 2, dc in ch at base of next dc, ch 2, dc in top of same dc; rep from **** 17 times more; ch 2, dc in ch at base of next dc, 2 dc around post of same dc, dc in top of same dc, 7 dc in next corner sp, dc in next dc on top edge of right square, 2 dc in next ch-2 sp; join with sl st in 3rd ch of beg ch-5.

Rnd 2: Ch 5, skip next 2 chs, dc in next dc; *ch 2, skip next 2 chs, dc in next dc*; rep from * to * 81 times more; **dc in next 5 dc, 2 dc in each of next 3 dc, dc in next 6 dc**; rep from * to * 37

times more; rep from ** to ** once; rep from * to
* 83 times more; rep from ** to ** once; rep from
* to * 37 times more; dc in next 5 dc, 2 dc in
each of next 3 dc, dc in next 5 dc; join with sl st
in 3rd ch of beg ch-5.

Rnd 3: Ch 5, skip next 2 chs, dc in next dc; *ch 2,
skip next 2 chs, dc in next dc*; rep from * to * 81
times more; **dc in next 6 dc, 2 dc in next of
next 4 dc, dc in next 7 dc**; rep from * to * 37
times more; rep from ** to ** once; rep from * to
* 83 times more; rep from ** to ** once; rep from
* to * 37 times more; dc in next 6 dc, 2 dc in
each of next 4 dc, dc in next 6 dc; join with sl st
in 3rd ch of beg ch-5. Finish off; weave in ends.

EDGING

Rnd 1: With right side facing, join cream with sl st
in last dc of top left corner dc group (22 dc at top
left corner); ch 3, 2 dc in same dc as joining, ch 6;
in each section of dc and ch-2 sps between corner
dc groups along left and right edges work: *skip
next dc, 3 dc in next dc, ch 6**; rep from * to **
17 times more; in each of 4 corner dc groups
work: 3 dc in 2nd dc of corner dc group, ch 6;
skip next 3 dc, 3 dc in next dc, ch 6*; rep
from *** to **** 4 times more; in each section of
dc and ch-2 sps between corner dc groups along
top and bottom edges work: rep from * to ** 41
times more; on final corner dc group, omit final
rep; join with sl st in 3rd ch of beg ch-3.

Rnd 2: Ch 3, dc in next 2 dc, ch 6; *dc in next 3
dc, ch 6; rep from * around; join with sl st in 3rd
ch of beg ch-3. Finish off; weave in ends.

Rnd 3: With right side facing, join lt green with sl
st in same ch as joining; ch 3, dc in next 2 dc, ch
3, sc in next ch-6 sp, ch 3; *dc in next 3 dc, ch 3,
sc in next ch-6 sp, ch 3; rep from * around; join
with sl st in 3rd ch of beg ch-3. Finish off; weave
in ends.

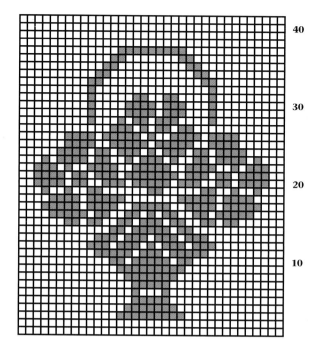

Floral Motif

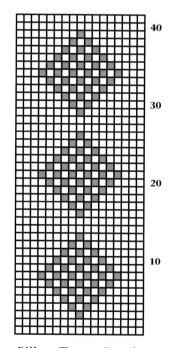

Pillow Topper Panel

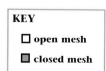

KEY
☐ open mesh
■ closed mesh

47

Flower Circles Tablecloth

Impressive 8-petal floral circles are separated by smaller four-leaf clover motifs in this gorgeous tablecloth.

SIZE: 48" x 55"

MATERIALS

Size 10 (bedspread weight) crochet thread
11 balls (400 yds each) or 4,400 yds cream
Size 8 (1.5 mm) steel crochet hook
  (or size required for gauge)

GAUGE

Large motif Rnds 1 through 3 = 3" diameter
Large motif Rnds 1 through 10 = 6³/4" diameter

SPECIAL STITCHES

Picot lp: Ch 10, sl st in 6th ch from hook, ch 4: picot lp made.

2 triple cluster (2 tr cl): *YO twice, insert hook in specified st or sp and draw up a lp, (YO and draw through 2 lps on hook) twice; rep from * once; YO and draw through all 3 lps on hook: 2 tr cl made.

3 triple cluster (3 tr cl): *YO twice, insert hook in specified st or sp and draw up a lp, (YO and draw through 2 lps on hook) twice; rep from * two times more; YO and draw through all 4 lps on hook: 3 tr cl made.

Dc decrease (dc dec): *YO, insert hook in specified st or sp and draw up a lp, YO and draw through 2 lps on hook; rep from * once; YO and draw through all 3 lps on hook: dc dec made.

Picot: Ch 3, sl st in 3rd ch from hook: picot made.

Instructions

LARGE MOTIF

(make 56)

First Motif

Ch 8; join with sl st to form a ring.

Rnd 1 (right side): Ch 3 (counts as dc), 23 dc in ring: 24 dc; join with sl st in 3rd ch of beg ch-3.

Rnd 2: Ch 1, sc in same ch as joining; *work picot lp, skip 2 dc**; sc in next dc; rep from * 6 times more; rep from * to ** once: 8 picot lps with 16 ch-4 sps; join with sl st in beg sc.

Rnd 3: *5 sc in next ch-4 sp; sl st in next picot; ch 4, 2 tr cl in same picot lp; (ch 5, 3 tr cl in same picot lp) 3 times; ch 5, 2 tr cl in same picot lp; ch 4, sl st in same picot lp; 5 sc in next ch-4 sp; rep from * 7 times more: 40 tr cl (8 groups with 5 tr cl in each) and 32 ch-5 sps; join with sl st in beg sc on Rnd 2.

Rnd 4: Sl st in next 5 sc, skip first ch of next ch-4, sl st in next 3 chs, sl st in top of tr cl, sl st in first 2 chs of next ch-5 sp, sc in next ch; *(ch 6, sc in next ch-5 sp) 3 times**; sc in next ch-5 sp on next 5 tr cl group; rep from * 6 times more; rep from * to ** once: 24 ch-6 sps; join with sl st in beg sc.

Rnd 5: Sl st in next 2 chs, 3 sc in same ch sp; *ch 6, 3 sc in next ch sp; rep from * around, ending with ch 2, tr in 2nd sl st to form last ch-6 sp: 24 ch-6 sps and 72 sc.

Rnd 6: Ch 4 (counts as tr now and through-out), 2 tr around post of joining tr; *(ch 5, 3 sc in next ch sp) 2 times, ch 5**; 3 tr in next ch sp; rep from * 6 times more; rep from * to ** once: 24 ch-5 sps, 24 tr and 48 sc; join with sl st in 4th ch of beg ch-4.

Rnd 7: Ch 4, 2 tr in same ch as joining; *ch 6, skip next tr, 3 tr in next tr, ch 6, skip next ch sp, 5 sc in next ch sp, ch 6, skip next ch sp**; 3 tr in next tr; rep from * 6 times more; rep from * to ** once: 48 tr, 24 ch-6 sps and 40 sc; join as before.

Rnd 8: Ch 4, tr in next 2 tr; *ch 6, 3 sc in next ch sp, ch 6, tr in next 3 tr, ch 6, skip next sc, sc in next 3 sc, ch 6**; tr in next 3 tr; rep from * 6 times more; rep from * to ** once: 48 tr, 32 ch-6 sps and 48 sc; join.

Rnd 9: Ch 4, tr in next 2 tr; *(ch 6, 3 sc in next ch sp) 2 times, ch 6, tr in next 3 tr, ch 6, skip next sc, sc in next sc, ch 6**; tr in next 3 tr; rep from * 6 times more; rep from * to ** once: 48 tr, 40 ch-6 sps and 56 sc; join.

Rnd 10: Ch 4, tr in next 2 tr; *(ch 7, 3 sc in next ch sp) 3 times, ch 7, tr in next 3 tr, skip next 2 ch sps**; tr in next 3 tr; rep from * 6 times more; rep from * to ** once: 48 tr, 32 ch-7 sps and 72 sc; join. Finish off; weave in ends.

Note: *Join motifs into 7 rows of 8 motifs each while working Rnd 10 with wrong sides of motifs together.*

Motif with One Side Joining

Rnds 1 through 9: Rep Rnds 1 through 9 on First Motif.

Rnd 10: Ch 4, tr in next 2 tr; *(ch 7, 3 sc in next ch sp) 3 times; ch 7, tr in next 3 tr, skip next 2 ch sps, tr in next 3 tr; rep from * 5 times more; (ch 7, 3 sc in next ch sp) 2 times; ch 3, sc in 2nd ch sp after 6 tr on Rnd 10 on adjacent motif, ch 3, 3 sc in next ch sp on current motif, ch 3, sc in first ch sp after 6 tr on Rnd 10 on same adjacent motif , ch 3, tr in next 3 tr on current motif, skip next 2 ch sps, tr in next 3 tr; (ch 3, sc in next ch

Large Motif

sp on same adjacent motif, ch 3, 3 sc in next ch sp on current motif) 2 times; ch 7, 3 sc in next ch sp, ch 7, tr in next 3 tr: 48 tr, 28 ch-7 sps, 4 joined ch sps and 76 sc; join. Finish off; weave in ends.

Motif with Two Side Joinings

Rnds 1 through 9: Rep Rnds 1 through 9 on First Motif.

Rnd 10: Ch 4, tr in next 2 tr; *(ch 7, 3 sc in next ch sp) 3 times; ch 7, tr in next 3 tr, skip next 2 ch sps, tr in next 3 tr; rep from * 3 times more; **(ch 7, 3 sc in next ch sp) 2 times; ch 3, sc in 2nd ch sp after 6 tr on Rnd 10 on adjacent motif, ch 3, 3 sc in next ch sp on current motif, ch 3, sc in first ch sp after 6 tr on Rnd 10 on same adjacent motif, ch 3, tr in next 3 tr on current motif, skip next 2 ch sps, tr in next 3 tr; (ch 3, sc in next ch sp on same adjacent motif, ch 3, 3 sc in next ch sp on current motif) 2 times; ch 7, 3 sc in next ch sp, ch 7, tr in next 3 tr, skip next 2 ch sps***; tr in next 3 tr; rep from ** to *** once:

48 tr, 24 ch-7 sps, 8 joined ch sps and 80 sc; join. Finish off; weave in ends.

Note: *Small motifs fill in corner spaces between large motifs. Last rnd on small motifs is joined to last rnd of 4 joined large motifs with wrong sides of motifs together.*

SMALL MOTIF

(make 42)

Ch 8; join with sl st to form a ring.

Rnd 1 (right side): *Ch 4, 2 tr cl in ring, ch 4, 3 sc in ring; rep from * 3 times more: four 2 tr cl, 8 ch-4 sps and 12 sc; join with sl st in first ch of beg ch-4.

Rnd 2: Sl st in next 3 chs, ch 3 (counts as dc now and throughout), 2 dc in same ch as last sl st; *ch 5, skip next 2 tr cl, 3 dc in next ch, ch 5, skip next 3 sc**; 3 dc in 4th ch of next ch-4; rep from * 2 times more; rep from * to ** once: 24 dc and 8 ch-5 sps; join with sl st in 3rd ch of beg ch-3.

Rnd 3: Ch 3, dc in next 2 dc; *ch 6, 3 sc in next ch sp, ch 6, dc in next 3 dc, ch 3, sc in next ch sp, ch 3**; dc in next 3 dc; rep from * 2 times more; rep from * to ** once: 24 dc, 8 ch-6 sps, 8 ch-3 sps and 16 sc; join as before.

Rnd 4: Ch 4 (counts as tr), tr in next 2 dc; *ch 3, sc in ch sp before 6 tr on Rnd 10 on adjacent large motif, ch 3, 3 sc in next ch sp on current motif; ch 3, sc in next ch sp on same adjacent large motif; ch 3, sc in 2nd ch sp after 6 tr on next adjacent large motif, ch 3, 3 sc in next ch sp on current motif; ch 3, sc in first ch sp after 6 tr on same adjacent large motif, ch 3**; tr in next 6 dc on current motif; rep from * 2 times more; rep from * to ** once; tr in next 3 dc on current motif; sl st in 4th ch of beg ch-4. Finish off; weave in ends.

Rnd 1: With right side facing, join with sl st in first joined ch sp on large motif before corner large motif, ch 2, dc in next joined ch sp on corner large motif, ch 3, 3 sc in next unjoined ch sp on same large motif; *ch 7, 3 sc in next unjoined ch sp on same large motif; rep from * to next large motif; ch 3**; dc dec in 2 joined ch sps on same and next large motifs; ch 3, 3 sc in next unjoined ch sp; rep from * around all 4 edges, ending at **; join with sl st in first dc.

Rnd 2: Ch 1, 2 sc in first ch-3 sp; *picot, ch 5, 2 sc in next ch-7 sp, picot, ch 5; **work [3 tr cl, (ch 1, picot, ch 1, 3 tr cl) 3 times] in next ch-7 sp over 6 tr on Rnd 10 of large motif; ch 5***; (2 sc in next ch-7 sp, picot, ch 5) 3 times; rep from ** 3 times more around corner large motif or once more along side large motif; rep from ** to *** once; 2 sc in next ch-7 sp, picot, ch 5, 2 sc in next ch-3 sp on same large motif, picot****; 2 sc in next ch-3 sp on next large motif; rep from * around all 4 edges, ending at ****; join with sl st in first sc. Finish off; weave in ends.

Floral Strips Bedspread

A pretty posy sprig centers each of the filet strips in this cloth, which is bordered on each side with a row of cabbage roses.

SIZE: 53¹/₂" x 93¹/₂" top plus 13¹/₂" overhangs on each side

MATERIALS

Size 10 crochet cotton,
   55 balls (350 yds each) or 19,250 yds white
Size 7 (1.65 mm) steel crochet hook
   (or size required for gauge)

GAUGE

14¹/₂ mesh = 4"; 18 mesh rows = 4"

Instructions

FLORAL STRIPS
(make 3)

Ch 199.

Row 1 (right side): Dc in 5th ch from hook, dc in next 2 chs, ch 2, skip 2 chs, dc in next 19 chs; (ch 2, skip 2 chs, dc in next ch) 3 times; dc in next 129 chs; (ch 2, skip 2 chs, dc in next ch) 3 times; dc in next 18 chs, ch 2, skip 2 chs, dc in last 4 chs: 8 open mesh and 57 closed mesh; ch 3, turn.

Rows 2 through 61: Work open and closed mesh as per chart and filet instructions on pages 134-138.

Rep Rows 2 through 61 six times more. At end of last row, finish off; weave in ends.

EDGINGS
(make 2)

Ch 118.

Row 1 (right side on right edging and wrong side on left edging): Dc in 5th ch from hook, dc in next 5 chs; (ch 2, skip 2 chs, dc in next ch) 2 times; *dc in next 3 chs, ch 2, skip 2 chs, dc in next ch, dc in next 3 chs*; (ch 2, skip 2 chs, dc in next ch) 4 times; rep from * to * once; (ch 2, skip 2 chs, dc in next ch) 11 times; dc in next 21 chs; (ch 2, skip 2 chs, dc in next ch) 5 times; dc in last 3 chs: 24 open mesh and 14 closed mesh; ch 3, turn.

Rows 2 through 49: Work open and closed mesh as per chart and filet instructions on pages 134-138.

Rep Rows 2 through 49 seven times more. Rep Rows 2 through 37 once. At end of last row, finish off; weave in ends.

With right sides facing, whip stitch 3 Floral Strips together with beg of each strip at bottom. Whip stitch left edging onto left edge of strips and right edging onto right edge of strips.

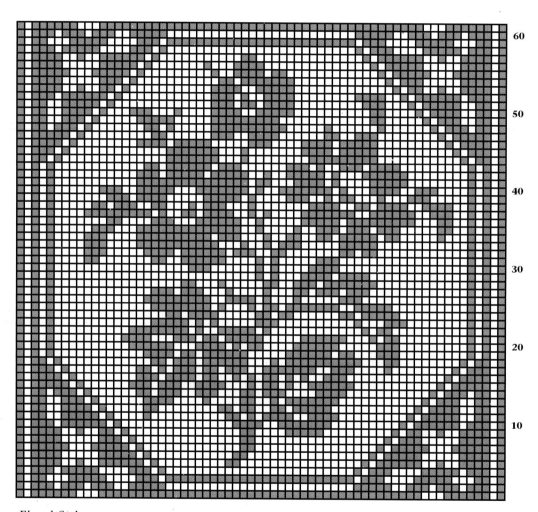

Floral Strips

KEY
☐ open mesh
■ closed mesh

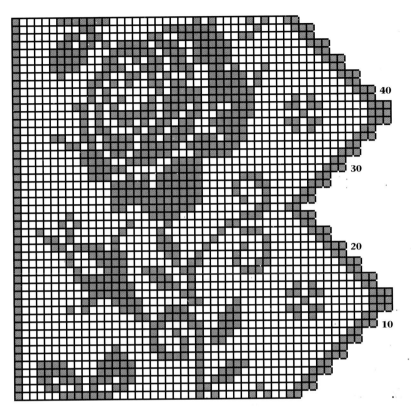

Edgings

40

30

20

10

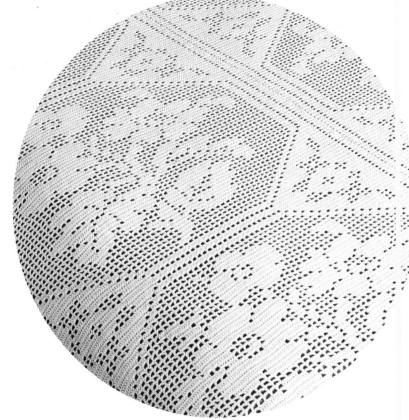

Colorful Floral Squares

Choose your favorite color for the flower centers of these innovative squares, or use a variety of colors. The lacy mesh background sets off the dimensional flowers perfectly for a cottage look.

SIZE: 63" x 70"

MATERIALS

Size 10 (bedspread weight) crochet thread
    16 balls (350 yds each) or 5,600 yds white
    4 balls (350 yds each) or 1,400 yds red
Size 5 (1.90 mm) steel crochet hook
    (or size required for gauge)

GAUGE

Motif = 7" square

Motif

Instructions

MOTIF
(make 90)

First Motif

With red, ch 6; join with sl st to form a ring.

Rnd 1 (right side): Ch 3 (counts as dc now and throughout), 23 dc in ring: 24 dc; join with sl st in 3rd ch of beg ch-3.

Rnd 2: Working in back lps only, sl st in next dc, ch 3, dc in next 2 dc, ch 12; *dc in same dc as last dc made, dc in next 3 dc, ch 12; rep from

56

* 6 times more; dc in same dc as joining: 32 dc and 8 ch-12 lps; join as before.

Rnd 3: Ch 1, sc in sp before next dc; *20 dc in next ch-12 lp, sc in sp between 2nd and 3rd dc of next 4 dc; rep from * 6 times more; 20 dc in next ch-12 lp; join with sl st in beg sc: 160 dc and 8 sc. Finish off; weave in ends.

Rnd 4: With right side facing, join white with sl st in sp bet 10th and 11th dc of any 20 dc group; ch 3, (3 dc, ch 3, 4 dc) in same sp; *ch 10, sc in sp bet 10th and 11th dc of next 20 dc group, ch 10**; (4 dc, ch 3, 4 dc) in sp bet 10th and 11th dc of next 20 dc group; rep from * 2 times more; rep from * to ** once: 32 dc, 4 sc, 4 ch-3 sps and 8 ch-10 lps; join with sl st in 3rd ch of beg ch-3.

Rnd 5: Sl st in next 3 dc and in next ch-3 sp, ch 3, (3 dc, ch 3, 4 dc) in same ch sp; *(ch 5, sc) twice in next ch-10 lp; rep from * once; ch 5**; (4 dc, ch 3, 4 dc) in next ch-3 sp; rep from * 2 times more; rep from * to ** once: 32 dc, 16 sc, 4 ch-3 sps and 20 ch-5 lps; join as before.

Rnd 6: Sl st in next 3 dc and in next ch-3 sp, ch 3, (3 dc, ch 3, 4 dc) in same ch sp; *(ch 5, sc in next ch-5 lp) 5 times, ch 5**; (4 dc, ch 3, 4 dc) in next ch-3 sp; rep from * 2 times more; rep from * to ** once: 32 dc, 20 sc, 4 ch-3 sps and 24 ch-5 lps; join.

Rnds 7 through 11: Rep Rnd 6 five times more, increasing underlined number by one in each rnd. At end of Rnd 11: 32 dc, 40 sc, 4 ch-3 sps and 44 ch-5 lps.

Rnd 12: Sl st in next 3 dc and in next ch-3 sp, ch 3, (3 dc, ch 3, 4 dc) in same ch sp, ch 1; * sc in next ch-5 lp, (5 dc, ch 3, 5 dc) in next ch-5 lp; rep from * 4 times more; sc in next ch-5 lp, ch 1**; (4 dc, ch 3, 4 dc) in next ch-3 sp, ch 1; rep from * 2 times more; rep from * to ** once: 232 dc, 24 sc and 24 ch-3 sps; join. Finish off; weave in ends.

Work remaining motifs same as First Motif through Rnd 11. Join motifs into 10 rows of 9 motifs each along one or two sides of Rnd 12 of each motif as follows:

Motif with One Side Joining

Rnd 12: Sl st in next 3 dc and in next ch-3 sp, ch 3, (3 dc, ch 3, 4 dc) in same ch sp, ch 1; *sc in next ch-5 lp, (5 dc, ch 3, 5 dc) in next ch-5 lp; rep from * 4 times more; sc in next ch-5 lp, ch 1**; (4 dc, ch 3, 4 dc) in next ch-3 sp; rep from * to ** once; 4 dc in next ch-3 sp, ch 1, sc in corresponding corner ch-3 sp on adjacent motif, ch 1, 4 dc in same ch-3 sp on current motif, ch 1; ***sc in next ch-5 lp, 5 dc in next ch-5 lp, ch 1, sc in corresponding ch-3 sp on adjacent motif, ch 1, 5 dc in same ch-5 lp on current motif; rep from *** 4 times more; sc in next ch-5 lp, ch 1, 4 dc in next ch-3 sp, ch 1, sc in corresponding corner ch-3 sp on adjacent motif, ch 1, 4 dc in same ch-3 sp on current motif, ch 1; rep from * to ** once: 232 dc, 24 sc, 17 ch-3 sps and 7 joined ch-3 sps; join. Finish off; weave in ends.

Motif with Two Side Joinings

Rnd 12: Sl st in next 3 dc and in next ch-3 sp, ch 3, (3 dc, ch 3, 4 dc) in same ch sp, ch 1; *sc in next ch-5 lp, (5 dc, ch 3, 5 dc) in next ch-5 lp; rep from * 4 times more; sc in next ch-5 lp, ch 1**; 4 dc in next ch-3 sp, ch 1, sc in corresponding corner ch-3 sp on adjacent motif, ch 1, 4 dc in same ch-3 sp on current motif, ch 1; ***sc in next ch-5 lp, 5 dc in next ch-5 lp, ch 1, sc in corresponding ch-3 sp on adjacent motif, ch 1, 5 dc in same ch-5 lp on current motif; rep from *** 4 times more; sc in next ch-5 lp, ch 1****; 4 dc in next ch-3 sp, ch 1, sc in corresponding joined corner ch-3 sp on adjacent motifs, ch 1, 4 dc in same ch-3 sp on current motif, ch 1; rep from *** to **** once; (4 dc, ch 3, 4 dc) in next ch-3 sp, ch 1; rep from * to ** once: 232 dc, 24 sc, 11 ch-3 sps and 13 joined ch-3 sps; join. Finish off; weave in ends.

Popcorn Diamonds Bedspread

Rich with texture, this spread is crafted with diamond motifs shaped with popcorn stitches. When joined, the motifs form a giant star design.

SIZE: 82" x 84"

MATERIALS

Size 3 crochet thread
   70 balls (150 yds each) or 10,500 yds natural
Size F (3.75 mm) crochet hook
   (or size required for gauge)

GAUGE

Rnds 1 through 3 = 3$1/2$" diameter
Full Motif = 10$1/2$" diameter between sides,
12" diameter between points

SPECIAL STITCHES

Popcorn (PC): Work 6 dc in specified sp, remove lp from hook, insert hook from front to back (if popcorn is worked on right side) or from back to front (if popcorn is worked on wrong side) in top of first of 6 dc, return lp to hook and pull lp through first dc: PC made.

Picot: Ch 3, sl st in top of last dc made: picot made.

Shell: Work [(dc, picot) 6 times, dc] in specified st: shell made.

Instructions

FULL HEXAGON MOTIF
(make 68)

Ch 6; join with sl st to form a ring.

Rnd 1 (right side): Ch 3 (counts as dc now and throughout), 17 dc in ring: 18 dc; join with sl st in 3rd ch of beg ch-3.

Rnd 2: Sl st in next dc, ch 3; (2 dc, ch 1, 3 dc) in same ch as joining; *skip next 2 dc, (3 dc, ch 1, 3 dc) in next dc; rep from * 4 times more; 36 dc and 6 ch-1 sps; join as before.

Rnd 3: Sl st in next 2 dc and in next ch-1 sp, ch 3; (2 dc, ch 1, 3 dc) in same ch-1 sp, ch 1; *(3 dc, ch 1, 3 dc) in next ch-1 sp, ch 1; rep from * 4 times more: 36 dc and 12 ch-1 sps; join.

Rnd 4: Sl st in next 2 dc and in next ch-1 sp, ch 3; (3 dc, ch 1, 4 dc) in same ch-1 sp; ch 1, dc in next ch-1 sp, ch 1; *(4 dc, ch 1, 4 dc) in next ch-1 sp; ch 1, dc in next ch-1 sp, ch 1; rep from * 4 times more: 54 dc and 18 ch-1 sps; join.

Rnd 5: Sl st in next 3 dc and in next ch-1 sp, ch 3; (3 dc, ch 1, 4 dc) in same ch-1 sp; *(ch 1, dc in next ch-1 sp) 2 times, ch 1**; (4 dc, ch 1, 4 dc) in next ch-1 sp; rep from * 5 times more, ending final rep at **: 60 dc and 24 ch-1 sps; join.

Rnd 6: Sl st in next 3 dc and in next ch-1 sp, ch 3; (3 dc, ch 1, 4 dc) in same ch-1 sp; *ch 1, dc in next ch-1 sp, ch 1, PC in next ch-1 sp, ch 1, dc in next ch-1 sp, ch 1**; (4 dc, ch 1, 4 dc) in next ch-1 sp; rep from * 5 times more, ending final rep at **: 60 dc, 6 PC and 30 ch-1 sps; join.

Full Hexagon Motif

Rnd 7: Sl st in next 3 dc and in next ch-1 sp, ch 3; (3 dc, ch 1, 4 dc) in same ch-1 sp; *ch 1, dc in next ch-1 sp, ch 1, PC in next ch-1 sp, ch 3; PC in next ch-1 sp, ch 1, dc in next ch-1 sp, ch 1**; (4 dc, ch 1, 4 dc) in next ch-1 sp; rep from * 5 times more, ending final rep at **: 60 dc, 12 PC, 6 ch-3 sps and 30 ch-1 sps; join.

Rnd 8: Sl st in next 3 dc and in next ch-1 sp, ch 3; (3 dc, ch 1, 4 dc) in same ch-1 sp; *ch 1, dc in next ch-1 sp, ch 1, PC in next ch-1 sp, ch 2; dc in each ch of next ch-3 sp, ch 2, PC in next ch-1 sp, ch 1, dc in next ch-1 sp, ch 1**; (4 dc, ch 1, 4 dc) in next ch-1 sp; rep from * 5 times more, ending final rep at **: 78 dc, 12 PC, 12 ch-2 sps and 30 ch-1 sps; join.

Rnd 9: Sl st in next 3 dc and in next ch-1 sp, ch 3; (3 dc, ch 1, 4 dc) in same ch-1 sp; *ch 1, dc in next ch-1 sp, ch 1, PC in next ch-1 sp, ch 2; dc in each ch of next ch-2 sp, dc in back lp of next 3 dc, dc in each ch of next ch-2 sp, ch 2; PC in next ch-1 sp, ch 1, dc in next ch-1 sp, ch 1**; (4 dc, ch 1, 4 dc) in next ch-1 sp; rep from * 5 times more, ending final rep at **: 102 dc, 12 PC, 12 ch-2 sps and 30 ch-1 sps; join.

Rnd 10: Sl st in next 3 dc and in next ch-1 sp, ch 3; (3 dc, ch 1, 4 dc) in same ch-1 sp; *ch 1, dc in next ch-1 sp, ch 1, PC in next ch-1 sp, ch 2; dc in each ch of next ch-2 sp, dc in back lp of next 7 dc, dc in each ch of next ch-2 sp, ch 2; PC in next ch-1 sp, ch 1, dc in next ch-1 sp, ch 1**; (4 dc, ch 1, 4 dc) in next ch-1 sp; rep from * 5 times more, ending final rep at **: 126 dc, 12 PC, 12 ch-2 sps and 30 ch-1 sps; join.

Rnd 11: Sl st in next 3 dc and in next ch-1 sp, ch 3; (3 dc, ch 1, 4 dc) in same ch-1 sp; *ch 1, dc in next ch-1 sp, ch 1, PC in next ch-1 sp, ch 2; dc in each ch of next ch-2 sp, dc in back lp of next 11 dc, dc in each ch of next ch-2 sp, ch 2; PC in next ch-1 sp, ch 1, dc in next ch-1 sp, ch 1**; (4 dc, ch 1, 4 dc) in next ch-1 sp; rep from * 5 times more, ending final rep at **: 150 dc, 12 PC, 12 ch-2 sps and 30 ch-1 sps; join. Finish off; weave in ends.

HALF HEXAGON MOTIF
(make 8)

Ch 4; join with sl st to form a ring.

Row 1 (wrong side): Ch 3 (counts as dc now and throughout), 10 dc in ring: 11 dc; ch 3 (counts as dc on next row), turn.

Row 2 (right side): Work (2 dc, ch 1, 3 dc) in first dc; *skip next 2 dc, (3 dc, ch 1, 3 dc) in next dc; rep from * 2 times more: 24 dc and 4 ch-1 sps; turn.

Row 3: Sl st in next 2 dc and in next ch-1 sp, ch 3; (2 dc, ch 1, 3 dc) in same ch-1 sp; *ch 1, (3 dc, ch 1, 3 dc) in next ch-1 sp; rep from * 2 times more: 24 dc and 7 ch-1 sps; turn.

Row 4: Sl st in next 2 dc and in next ch-1 sp, ch 3; (3 dc, ch 1, 4 dc) in same ch-1 sp; *ch 1, dc in next ch-1 sp, ch 1; (4 dc, ch 1, 4 dc) in next ch-1 sp; rep from * 2 times more: 35 dc and 10 ch-1 sps; turn.

Half Hexagon Motif

Row 5: Sl st in next 3 dc and in next ch-1 sp, ch 3; (3 dc, ch 1, 4 dc) in same ch-1 sp; *(ch 1, dc in next ch-1 sp) 2 times, ch 1; (4 dc, ch 1, 4 dc) in next ch-1 sp; rep from * 2 times more: 38 dc and 13 ch-1 sps; turn.

Row 6: Sl st in next 3 dc and in next ch-1 sp, ch 3; (3 dc, ch 1, 4 dc) in same ch-1 sp; *ch 1, dc in next ch-1 sp, ch 1, PC in next ch-1 sp, ch 1, dc in next ch-1 sp, ch 1; (4 dc, ch 1, 4 dc) in next ch-1 sp; rep from * 2 times more: 38 dc, 3 PC and 16 ch-1 sps; turn.

Row 7: Sl st in next 3 dc and in next ch-1 sp, ch 3; (3 dc, ch 1, 4 dc) in same ch-1 sp; *ch 1, dc in next ch-1 sp, ch 1, PC in next ch-1 sp, ch 3; PC in next ch-1 sp, ch 1, dc in next ch-1 sp, ch 1; (4 dc, ch 1, 4 dc) in next ch-1 sp; rep from * 2 times more: 38 dc, 6 PC, 3 ch-3 sps and 16 ch-1 sps; turn.

Row 8: Sl st in next 3 dc and in next ch-1 sp, ch 3; (3 dc, ch 1, 4 dc) in same ch-1 sp; *ch 1, dc in next ch-1 sp, ch 1, PC in next ch-1 sp, ch 2; dc in each ch of next ch-3 sp, ch 2, PC in next ch-1 sp, ch 1; dc in next ch-1 sp, ch 1; (4 dc, ch 1, 4 dc) in next ch-1 sp; rep from * 2 times more: 47 dc, 6 PC, 6 ch-2 sps and 16 ch-1 sps; turn.

Row 9: Sl st in next 3 dc and in next ch-1 sp, ch 3; (3 dc, ch 1, 4 dc) in same ch-1 sp; *ch 1, dc in next ch-1 sp, ch 1, PC in next ch-1 sp, ch 2; dc in each ch of next ch-2 sp, dc in front lp of next 3 dc, dc in each ch of next ch-2 sp, ch 2; PC in next ch-1 sp, ch 1, dc in next ch-1 sp, ch 1; (4 dc, ch 1, 4 dc) in next ch-1 sp; rep from * 2 times more: 59 dc, 6 PC, 6 ch-2 sps and 16 ch-1 sps; turn.

Row 10: Sl st in next 3 dc and in next ch-1 sp, ch 3; (3 dc, ch 1, 4 dc) in same ch-1 sp; *ch 1, dc in next ch-1 sp, ch 1, PC in next ch-1 sp, ch 2; dc in each ch of next ch-2 sp, dc in back lp of next 7 dc, dc in each ch of next ch-2 sp, ch 2; PC in next ch-1 sp, ch 1, dc in next ch-1 sp; (4 dc, ch 1, 4 dc) in next ch-1 sp; rep from * 2 times more: 71 dc, 6 PC, 6 ch-2 sps and 16 ch-1 sps; turn.

Row 11: Sl st in next 3 dc and in next ch-1 sp, ch 3; (3 dc, ch 1, 4 dc) in same ch-1 sp; *ch 1, dc in next ch-1 sp, ch 1, PC in next ch-1 sp, ch 2; dc in each ch of next ch-2 sp, dc in front lp of next 11 dc, dc in each ch of next ch-2 sp, ch 2; PC in next ch-1 sp, ch 1, dc in next ch-1 sp, ch 1; (4 dc, ch 1, 4 dc) in next ch-1 sp; rep from * 2 times more: 83 dc, 6 PC, 6 ch-2 sps and 16 ch-1 sps. Finish off; weave in ends.

ASSEMBLY

With right sides together, join motifs together into 5 vertical rows with 8 full motifs in each row and 4 vertical rows with 7 full motifs and 1 half motif at each end of row by working a sl st in back lp of each st along one edge of motifs. With right sides together, join vertical rows together, alternating rows of 8 full motifs and rows of 7 full/2 half motifs, starting and ending with rows of 8 full motifs by working a sl st in back lp of each st along edge of motifs in rows (see Assembly Diagram).

EDGING

With right side facing, join with sl st in ch-1 sp at top joining of 1st and 2nd vertical rows of motifs; *skip next 3 dc, shell in next dc; skip next ch-1 sp and next dc, sl st in next ch-1 sp; skip next PC and next ch-2 sp, shell in next dc; **skip next 3 dc, sl st in next dc; skip next 2 dc, shell in next dc; rep from ** once more; skip next ch-2 sp and next PC, sl st in next ch-1 sp; skip next dc and next ch-1 sp, shell in next dc; skip next 3 dc, sl st in next ch-1 sp; rep from * along unjoined edges of first vertical row of motifs on left edge of bedspread, working sl st in joined ch-1 sps at motif joinings and ending at bottom joining of 1st and 2nd vertical rows of motifs: 90 shells. Finish off; weave in ends. With right side facing, rep edging along last vertical row of motifs on right edge of bedspread, starting at bottom joining of 8th and 9th vertical rows of motifs and ending at top joining of 8th and 9th vertical rows of motifs: 90 shells. Finish off; weave in ends.

64

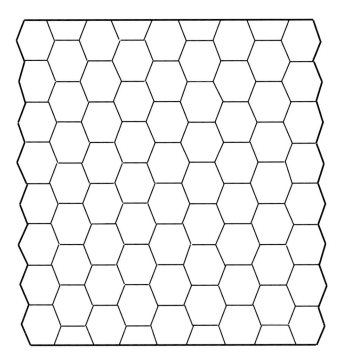

Assembly Diagram

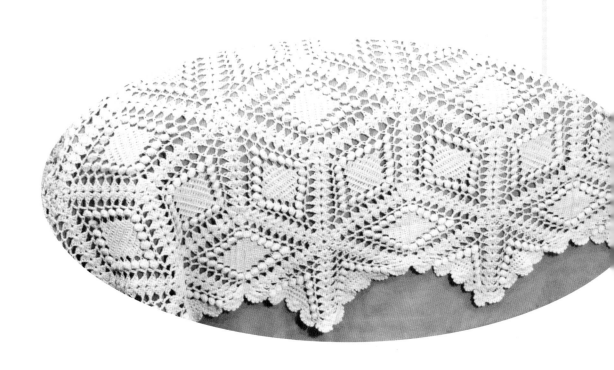

God Bless Our Home Tablecloth

Honor your home with this beautiful filet cloth that sets the stage for an elegant family dinner. Fringe all around the edge adds the final touch to this piece, which is sure to become an heirloom.

SIZE: 65" x 51" plus fringe

MATERIALS

Size 10 crochet cotton,
 15 balls (400 yds each) or 6,000 yds natural
Size 5 (1.90 mm) steel crochet hook
 (or size required for gauge)

GAUGE

9 mesh = 4^{1}/4"; 12 mesh rows = 4^{1}/4"

STITCH GUIDE

Extended dc (edc): YO, insert hook in specified st and draw up a lp, YO and draw through one lp on hook, (YO and draw through 2 lps on hook) twice: edc made.

To join with edc: Make slip knot and place on hook, YO, insert hook in back lp of first edc of previous row and draw up a lp, YO and draw through one lp on hook, (YO and draw through 2 lps on hook) twice: join with edc made.

Open Mesh: Ch 3, skip next 3 sts, edc in back lp (and lp below back lp for stability) of next st (see diagram): open mesh made.

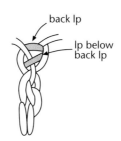

back lp

lp below back lp

Closed Mesh: Edc in back lp of next 4 sts: closed mesh made.

Notes: *Each row has a total of 131 open and closed mesh. All mesh are worked with 4 edc (or 3 chs and one edc) instead of 3 dc (or 2 chs and one dc), as in traditional filet crochet. All dark squares on chart are worked as closed mesh. All light squares on chart are worked as open mesh. Begin and end each row, working each row on right side. At end of Row 136, weave in all ends.*

Instructions

Ch 528.

Row 1 (right side): Edc in 5th ch from hook (skipped chs count as first edc), edc in next ch and in each ch across: 525 edc (131 closed mesh). Finish off.

Row 2: With right side facing, join with edc in back lp and back bar of first skipped ch of foundation ch, edc in back lp of next 4 edc (closed mesh made); *ch 3, skip next 3 edc, edc in back lp (and lp below back lp) of next edc (open mesh made); rep from * across to last 4 edc; edc in back lp of last 4 edc (closed mesh made): 2 closed mesh and 129 open mesh. Finish off.

Rows 3 through 136: With right side facing, join with edc, work open and closed mesh as per chart and Stitch Guide. Finish off.

EDGING

Rnd 1: With right side facing, join with sl st in top right-hand corner, ch 6 (counts as edc and ch-3

sp), edc in same st as joining;
*ch 3, skip next
3 edc, edc in next edc; rep
from * across to next corner;
work (edc, ch 3, edc) in next
corner; **ch 3, edc in top of
next row; rep from ** across
to next corner***; work (edc,
ch 3, edc) in next corner; rep
from * across other 2 edges,
ending at ***; ch 3: 538 edc
and 538 ch-3 sps; join with sl
st in 3rd ch of beg ch-6.

Rnd 2: Sl st in next corner
ch-3 sp, ch 7 (counts as edc
and ch-4 sp), edc in same
ch-3 sp; *ch 4, edc in next
ch-3 sp; rep from * around,
working (edc, ch 4, edc) in
each of next 3 corner ch-3
sps; ch 4: 542 edc and 542
ch-4 sps; join with sl st in 3rd
ch of beg ch-7.

Rnd 3: Sl st in next ch-4 sp,
ch 10 (counts as edc and
ch-7 sp), edc in next ch-4 sp;
*ch 7, edc in next ch-4 sp;
rep from * around; ch 7; 542
edc and 542 ch-7 sps; join
with sl st in 3rd ch of beg
ch-10. Finish off; weave
in ends.

FRINGE

Following Fringe Instructions
on page 142, cut 8" long
strand of thread. Knot 4
strands in each ch-7 sp
on Rnd 3 of Edging. Trim
if desired.

Chart—Left Half

130

120

110

100

90

80

70

60

50

40

30

20

10

Chart—Right Half

Elegance Bedspread

Elegant floral blocks make this lovely bedspread very special. Choose a flower color that matches or accents your décor to make a strong statement.

SIZE: 73" x 83"

MATERIALS

Size 10 (bedspread weight) crochet thread
 5 balls (350 yds each) or 1,750 yds blue
 18 balls (400 yds each) or 7,200 yds white
Size 5 (1.90 mm) steel crochet hook
 (or size required for gauge)

GAUGE

Motif Rnds 1 through 4 = $2^7/8$" diameter
Full motif = 10" square

SPECIAL STITCHES

Extended dc (edc): YO, insert hook in specified st and draw up a lp, YO and draw through one lp on hook, (YO and draw through 2 lps on hook) 2 times: edc made.

Sc decrease (sc dec): Insert hook in first specified ch-lp and draw up a lp, insert hook in second specified ch-lp and draw up a lp, YO and draw through all 3 lps on hook: sc dec made.

Beginning edc cluster (beg edc CL): Ch 3; *YO, insert hook in next st and draw up a lp, YO and draw through one lp on hook, YO and draw through 2 lps on hook; rep from * once more; YO and draw through all 3 lps on hook: beg edc CL made.

Edc cluster (edc CL): YO, insert hook in first specified st and draw up a lp, YO and draw through one lp on hook, YO and draw through 2 lps on hook; *YO, insert hook in next specified st and draw up a lp, YO and draw through one lp on hook, YO and draw through 2 lps on hook; rep from * once more; YO and draw through all 4 lps on hook: edc CL made.

Instructions

FIRST MOTIF

With blue, ch 8; join with sl st to form a ring.

Rnd 1 (right side): Ch 3 (counts as edc now and throughout), 19 edc in ring: 20 edc; join with sl st in 3rd ch of beg ch-3.

Rnd 2: Ch 3, edc in next edc, ch 2; *edc in next 2 edc, ch 2; rep from * around: 20 edc and 10 ch-2 sps; join as before.

Rnd 3: Sl st in next edc and in next ch-2 sp, ch 3, (edc, ch 3, 2 edc) in same ch-2 sp; *(2 edc, ch 3, 2 edc) in next ch-2 sp; rep from * around: 40 edc and 10 ch-3 sps; join.

Rnd 4: Sl st in next edc and in next ch-3 sp, ch 3, 7 edc in same ch-3 sp; *8 edc in next ch-3 sp; rep from * around: 80 edc; join. Finish off; weave in ends.

Rnd 5: With right side facing, join white with sl st in 3rd edc worked on Rnd 4, ch 3, edc in next edc, ch 10; *skip next 6 edc, edc in next 2 edc, ch 10; rep from * around: 20 edc and 10 ch-10 lps; join.

Rnd 6: Sl st in next edc and in next ch, ch 5 (counts as edc and ch-2 sp now and throughout); *skip next 2 sts, edc in next ch, ch 2; rep from * around: 40 edc and 40 ch-2 sps; join with sl st in 3rd ch of beg ch-5.

Rnd 7: Sl st in next ch-2 sp; ch 11 (counts as edc and ch-8 lp); *skip next ch-2 sp, edc in next ch-2 sp, ch 8; rep from * around: 20 edc and 20 ch-8 lps; join with sl st in 3rd ch of beg ch-11.

Rnd 8: Ch 5; *skip next 2 chs, edc in next st, ch 2; rep from * around: 60 edc and 60 ch-2 sps; join with sl st in 3rd ch of beg ch-5.

Rnd 9: Ch 3, 2 edc in next ch-2 sp; *edc in next edc, 2 edc in next ch-2 sp; rep from * around: 180 edc; join with sl st in 3rd ch of beg ch-3.

Rnd 10: Ch 4 (counts as edc and ch-1 sp now and throughout); *(skip next edc, edc in next edc, ch 1) 9 times; skip next edc, edc in next edc; ch 6, skip next 3 edc, (edc, ch 2, edc) in next edc; **ch 7, skip next 3 edc, (edc, ch 2, edc) in next edc; rep from ** 3 times more***; ch 6, skip next 4 edc, edc in next edc, ch 1; rep from * 3 times more, ending final rep at ***; ch 2, tr in 3rd ch of beg ch-4 (counts as ch-6 lp now and throughout): 84 edc, 16 ch-7 lps, 8 ch-6 lps, 20 ch-2 sps and 40 ch-1 sps.

Rnd 11: Ch 4, (edc, ch 1) 2 times around post of tr; *(edc in next ch-1 sp, ch 1) 10 times; (edc, ch 1, edc, ch 1, edc) in next ch-lp; ch 6, (edc, ch 2, edc) in next ch-lp; ch 7, (edc, ch 2, edc) in next ch-lp; ch 9, (edc, ch 2, edc) in next ch-lp; ch 7, (edc, ch 2, edc) in next ch-lp**; ch 6, (edc, ch 1) 3 times in next ch-lp; rep from * 3 times more, ending final rep at **; ch 2, tr in 3rd ch of beg ch-4: 96 edc, 4 ch-9 lps, 8 ch-7 lps, 8 ch-6 lps, 16 ch-2 sps and 60 ch-1 sps.

Rnd 12: Ch 4, (edc, ch 1) 2 times around post of tr; *(edc in next ch-1 sp, ch 1) 15 times; (edc, ch 1, edc, ch 1, edc) in next ch-lp; ch 6, (edc, ch 2, edc) in next ch-lp; [ch 7, (edc, ch 2, edc) in next ch-lp] 2 times**; ch 6, (edc, ch 1) 3 times in next ch-lp; rep from * 3 times more, ending final rep at **; ch 2, tr in 3rd ch of beg ch-4: 108 edc, 8 ch-7 lps, 8 ch-6 lps, 12 ch-2 sps and 80 ch-1 sps.

Rnd 13: Ch 4, (edc, ch 1) 2 times around post of tr; *(edc in next ch-1 sp, ch 1) 20 times; (edc, ch 1, edc, ch 1, edc) in next ch-lp, ch 6; (edc, ch 2, edc) in next ch-lp, ch 9; (edc, ch 2, edc) in next ch-lp**; ch 6, (edc, ch 1) 3 times in next ch-lp; rep from * 3 times more, ending final rep at **; ch 2, tr in 3rd ch of beg ch-4: 120 edc, 4 ch-9 lps, 8 ch-6 lps, 8 ch-2 sps and 100 ch-1 sps.

Rnd 14: Ch 4, (edc, ch 1) 2 times around post of tr; *(edc in next ch-1 sp, ch 1) 25 times; (edc, ch 1, edc, ch 1, edc) in next ch-lp, ch 7, (edc, ch 4, edc) in 5th ch of next ch-9 lp**; ch 7, (edc, ch 1) 3 times in next ch-lp; rep from * 3 times more, ending final rep at **; ch 7: 132 edc, 8 ch-7 lps, 4 ch-4 sps and 120 ch-1 sps; join with sl st in 3rd ch of beg ch-4.

Rnd 15: Ch 3; *(edc in next ch-1 sp, edc in next edc) 30 times; 6 edc in next ch-7 lp, (2 edc, 2 tr, ch 2, 2 tr, 2 edc) in next ch-4 sp, 6 edc in next ch-7 lp**; edc in next edc; rep from * 3 times more, ending final rep at **: 16 tr, 308 edc and 4 ch-2 sps. Finish off; weave in ends.

Rnd 16: With right side facing, join blue with sc in any corner ch-2 sp; *ch 5, skip next 2 tr, sc in next edc; (ch 5, skip next 3 edc, sc in next edc) 19 times; ch 5, skip next 2 tr**; (sc, ch 5, sc) in next corner ch-2 sp; rep from * 3 times more, ending final rep at **; sc in next corner ch-2 sp, ch 5: 88 edc and 88 ch-5 lps; join with sl st in beg sc. Finish off; weave in ends.

Note: With right sides facing, join motifs with one or two side joinings into 8 rows of 7 motifs each.

First Motif

Rnds 1 through 15: Rep Rnds 1 through 15 on First Motif.

Rnd 16: With right side facing, join blue with sc in any corner ch-2 sp; *ch 5, skip next 2 tr, sc in next edc; (ch 5, skip next 3 edc, sc in next edc) 19 times; ch 5, skip next 2 tr**; (sc, ch 5, sc) in next corner ch-2 sp; rep from * 2 times more, ending final rep at **; sc in next corner ch-2 sp, ch 2, sc in corresponding corner ch-5 lp on adjacent motif, ch 2, sc in same corner ch-2 sp on current motif; ch 2, sc in corresponding ch-5 lp on adjacent motif, ch 2, skip next 2 tr on current motif, sc in next edc on current motif; (ch 2, sc in corresponding ch-5 lp on adjacent motif, ch 2, skip next 3 edc on current motif, sc in next edc on current motif) 19 times; ch 2, sc in corresponding ch-5 lp on adjacent motif, ch 2, skip next 2 tr on current motif, sc in next corner ch-2 sp on current motif; ch 2, sc in corresponding corner ch-5 lp on adjacent motif, ch 2: 88 sc, 65 ch-5 lps and 23 joined ch-5 lps; join with sl st in beg sc. Finish off; weave in ends.

Rnds 1 through 15: Rep Rnds 1 through 15 on First Motif.

Rnd 16: With right side facing, join blue with sc in any corner ch-2 sp; *ch 5, skip next 2 tr, sc in next edc, (ch 5, skip next 3 edc, sc in next edc) 19 times; ch 5, skip next 2 tr**; (sc, ch 5, sc) in next corner ch-2 sp; rep from * to ** once; sc in next corner ch-2 sp, ch 2, sc in corresponding corner ch-5 lp on adjacent motif, ch 2, sc in same corner ch-2 sp on current motif; ***ch 2, sc in corresponding ch-5 lp on adjacent motif, ch 2, skip next 2 tr on current motif, sc in next edc on current motif; (ch 2, sc in corresponding ch-5 lp on adjacent motif, ch 2, skip next 3 edc on current motif, sc in next edc on current motif) 19 times; ch 2, sc in corresponding ch-5 lp on adjacent motif, ch 2, skip next 2 tr on current motif, sc in next corner ch-2 sp on current motif****; ch 2, sc in corresponding joined corner ch-5 lp on adjacent joined motifs, ch 2, sc in same corner ch-2 sp on current motif; rep from *** to **** once on second adjacent motif; ch 2, sc in corresponding corner ch-5 lp on second adjacent motif, ch 2: 88 sc, 43 ch-5 lps and 45 joined ch-5 lps; join with sl st in beg sc. Finish off; weave in ends.

EDGING

Rnd 1: With right side facing, join blue with sl st in any corner ch-5 lp, ch 3, (3 edc, ch 7, 4 edc) in same corner ch-5 lp; *ch 6, sc in next ch-5 lp; rep from * across side to next corner ch-5 lp; ch 6**; (4 edc, ch 7, 4 edc) in next corner ch-5 lp; rep from * 3 times more, ending final rep at **; sl st in 3rd ch of beg ch-3.

Rnd 2: Sl st in next 3 edc and in next 2 chs of corner ch-7 lp; (ch 6, sc, ch 7, sc, ch 6, sc) in same corner ch-7 lp; *ch 6, sc in next ch-6 lp; rep from * across side to next corner ch-7 lp, ch 6**; (sc, ch 6, sc, ch 7, sc, ch 6, sc) in next corner ch-7 lp; rep from * 3 times more, ending final rep at **; sl st in first sc. Finish off; weave in ends.

Rnd 3: With right side facing, join white with sl st in corner ch-7 lp before side with 8 motifs; ch 3, (3 edc, ch 5, 4 edc) in same corner ch-7 lp; *ch 4, (sc in next ch-6 lp, ch 6) 2 times, sc in next ch-6 lp, ch 4, 5 edc in next ch-6 lp**; rep from * to ** across side, ending in 4th ch-6 lp before next corner ch-7 lp; ch 4, (sc in next ch-6 lp, ch 6) 2 times, sc in next ch-6 lp, ch 4, (4 edc, ch 5, 4 edc) in next corner ch-7 lp; rep from * to ** across side, ending in 18th ch-6 lp before next corner ch-7 lp; ***ch 4, (sc in next ch-6 lp, ch 6) 2 times, sc dec in next 2 ch-6 lps, ch 4, 5 edc in next ch-6 lp; ch 4, (sc in next ch-6 lp, ch 6) 2 times, sc in next ch-6 lp, ch 4***; 5 edc in next ch-6 lp; rep from *** to *** once****; (4 edc, ch 5, 4 edc) in next corner ch-7 lp; rep from * across next 2 sides, ending at ****; join with sl st in 3rd ch of beg ch-3.

Rnd 4: Ch 3, edc in next 3 edc, 7 edc in corner ch-5 lp, edc in next 4 edc; *ch 4, skip next ch-4 sp, sc in next ch-6 lp, ch 6, sc in next ch-6 lp, ch 4**; (2 edc in next edc) 2 times, 3 edc in next edc, (2 edc in next edc) 2 times; rep from * across side; rep from * to ** once***; edc in next 4 edc, 7 edc in corner ch-5 lp, edc in next 4 edc; rep from * 3 times more, ending final rep at ***; join as before.

Rnd 5: Work beg edc CL; *ch 7, edc CL in next 3 edc, ch 7; (edc CL in same edc as end of last edc CL and in next 2 edc, ch 7) 3 times, edc CL in next 3 edc; **ch 4, skip next ch-4 sp, sc in next ch-6 lp, ch 4, (edc CL in next 3 edc, ch 7) 2 times, edc CL in same edc as end of last edc CL and in next 2 edc, ch 7, edc CL in next 3 edc; rep from ** across side; ch 4, skip next ch-4 sp, sc in next ch-6 lp; ch 4***; edc CL in next 3 edc; rep from * around, ending final rep at ***; join with sl st in top of beg edc CL. Finish off; weave in ends.

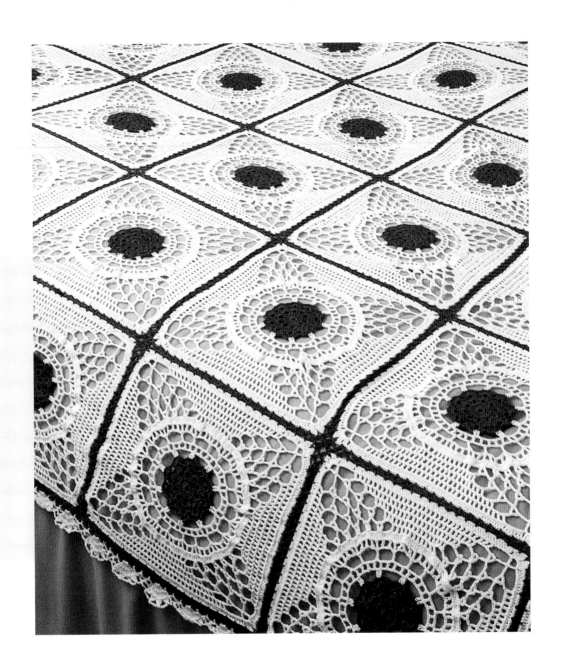

Oval Filet Tablecloth

Garlands of flowers surround the center and edges of this sweet oval cloth, done in filet.

SIZE: 38" x 49"

MATERIALS

Size 20 crochet thread
    8 balls (400 yds each) or 3,200 yds ecru
Size 9 (1.40 mm) steel crochet hook
    (or size required for gauge)
Spray starch (optional)

GAUGE

17 mesh = 4"
17 mesh rows = 4"

SPECIAL STITCHES

Triple triple (tr tr): YO 4 times, insert hook in specified st and draw up a lp, (YO and draw through 2 lps on hook) 4 times: tr tr made.

Instructions

Starting at bottom, ch 33.

Row 1 (right side): Dc in 9th ch from hook (skipped chs count as dc and ch-2 sp); *ch 2, skip 2 chs, dc in next ch; rep from * across: 9 open mesh; ch 17, turn.

Row 2: Dc in 9th ch from hook (skipped chs count as dc and ch-2 sp); ch 2, skip 2 chs, dc in next ch) 2 times; ch 2, skip 2 chs, dc in next dc; (2 dc in next ch-2 sp, dc in next dc) 8 times; 2 dc in next ch-sp, dc in 3rd skipped ch at beg of Row 1, ch 2, tr tr in same ch as last dc; (ch 2, tr tr in middle of post of last tr tr made) 3 times: 8 open mesh and 9 closed mesh; ch 11, turn.

Rows 3 through 106: Work open and closed filet mesh as per chart and filet instructions on pages 134-138.

Rows 107 through 211: Turn chart upside down and work Rows 1 through 105 in reverse order, skipping Row 106. At end of Row 211, finish off; weave in ends.

EDGING

With right side facing, join with sc in any ch-2 sp on edge of tablecloth, work sc evenly around entire edge, working 2 sc in each ch-2 sp and around post of each dc, 1 sc in each dc and in ch at base of each dc, and 5 sc in each corner inc or dec sp. Join with sl st in first sc. Finish off; weave in ends.

Lightly apply spray starch following manufacturer's directions, if desired.

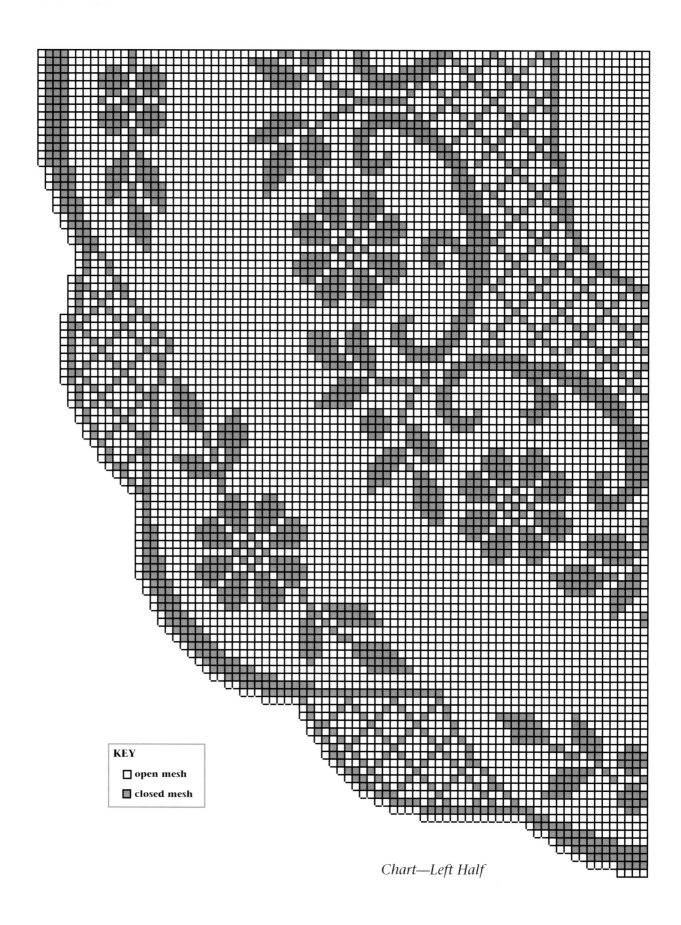

KEY
□ open mesh
■ closed mesh

Chart—Left Half

Chart—Right Half

Rosy Table Topper

Top off a round table with this easy and quick-to-make topper featuring a band of roses around its outer edges and in the center.

SIZE: 68" diameter

MATERIALS
Size 3 crochet thread
  11 balls (150 yds each) or 1,650 yds red
Size F (3.75 mm) crochet hook
  (or size required for gauge)
Stitch markers

GAUGE
Rnds 1 through 4 = 5^1/$_2$" diameter

SPECIAL STITCHES

Beginning 7 double triple decrease (beg 7 dtr dec): Ch 5, YO 3 times, insert hook in first specified st and draw up a lp, (YO and draw through 2 lps on hook) 3 times; *YO 3 times, insert hook in next specified st and draw up a lp, (YO and draw through 2 lps on hook) 3 times; rep from * 4 times more; YO and draw through all 7 lps on hook: beg 7 dtr dec made.

7 double triple decrease (7 dtr dec): YO 3 times, insert hook in first specified st and draw up a lp, (YO and draw through 2 lps on hook) 3 times; *YO 3 times, insert hook in next specified st and draw up a lp, (YO and draw through 2 lps on hook) 3 times; rep from * 5 times more; YO and draw through all 8 lps on hook: 7 dtr dec made.

Beginning 6 triple decrease (beg 6 tr dec): Ch 4, YO 2 times, insert hook in first specified st and draw up a lp, (YO and draw through 2 lps on hook) 2 times; *YO 2 times, insert hook in next specified st and draw up a lp, (YO and draw through 2 lps on hook) 2 times; rep from * 3 times more; YO and draw through all 6 lps on hook: beg 6 tr dec made.

6 triple decrease (6 tr dec): YO 2 times, insert hook in first specified st and draw up a lp, (YO and draw through 2 lps on hook) 2 times; *YO 2 times, insert hook in next specified st and draw up a lp, (YO and draw through 2 lps on hook) 2 times; rep from * 4 times more; YO and draw through all 7 lps on hook: 6 tr dec made.

Triple triple (tr tr): YO 4 times, insert hook in specified st and draw up a lp, (YO and draw through 2 lps on hook) 5 times: tr tr made.

Instructions

FLOWER MOTIF RING
(WITH 24 FLOWER MOTIFS)

First Flower Motif

Ch 5; join with sl st to form a ring.

Rnd 1 (right side): Ch 8 (counts as tr and ch-4 lp); *tr in ring, ch 4; rep from * 5 times more: 7 tr and 7 ch-4 lps; join with sl st in 4th ch of beg ch-7.

Rnd 2: Sl st in first ch-4 lp, ch 4 (counts as tr), 5 tr in same ch-4 lp, ch 1; *6 tr in next ch-4 lp, ch 1; rep from * around: 42 tr and 7 ch-1 lps; join with sl st in 4th ch of beg ch-4.

Rnd 3: Ch 3 (counts as dc), dc in next 5 tr, ch 4; *dc in next 6 tr, ch 4; rep from * around: 42 dc and 7 ch-4 lps; join with sl st in 3rd ch of beg ch-3.

Rnd 4: Work beg 6 tr dec in next 5 dc; *ch 8, sc in next ch-4 lp**; ch 8, 6 tr dec in next 6 dc; rep from * around, ending final rep at **; ch 4, join with tr in top of beg 6 tr dec: seven 6 tr dec, 7 sc and 14 ch-8 lps.

Rnd 5: Ch 1, 2 sc around post of joining tr, ch 8; *2 sc in next ch-8 lp, ch 8; rep from * around: 28 sc and 14 ch-8 lps; join with sl st in first sc. Finish off; weave in ends.

Note: *When joining Flower Motifs, make sure right sides of Flower Motifs are facing.*

2nd through 23rd Flower Motifs

Ch 5; join with sl st to form a ring.

Rnds 1 through 4: Rep Rnds 1 through 4 on First Flower Motif.

Rnd 5: Ch 1, 2 sc around post of joining tr, ch 8; *2 sc in next ch-8 lp, ch 8; rep from * 10 times more; sc in 8th ch-8 lp on previous Flower Motif, ch 3, sc in 5th ch of last ch-8 (place marker in skipped ch-sp), ch 4, 2 sc in next ch-8 lp on current Flower Motif; ch 4, 2 sc in 7th ch-8 lp on same previous Flower Motif, ch 4, 2 sc in next ch-8 lp on current Flower Motif; ch 8, sc in 6th ch-8 lp on same previous Flower Motif; ch 3, sc in 5th ch of last ch-8, ch 4; join with sl st in first sc. Finish off; weave in ends.

24th Flower Motif

Ch 5; join with sl st to form a ring.

Rnds 1 through 4: Rep Rnds 1 through 4 on First Flower Motif.

Rnd 5: Ch 1, 2 sc around post of joining tr, ch 8; *2 sc in next ch-8 lp, ch 8; rep from * 3 times more; ch 8, sc in 14th ch-8 lp on First Flower Motif; ch 3, sc in 5th ch of last ch-8, ch 4, 2 sc in next ch-8 lp on current Flower Motif; ch 4, 2 sc in 13th ch-8 lp on First Flower Motif, ch 4, 2 sc in

next ch-8 lp on current Flower Motif; ch 8, sc in 12th ch-8 lp on First Flower Motif, ch 3, sc in 5th ch of last ch-8 (place marker in skipped ch-sp), ch 4, *sc in next ch-8 lp on current Flower Motif, ch 8) 4 times; sc in 8th ch-8 lp on 23rd Flower Motif, ch 3, sc in 5th ch of last ch-8 (place marker in skipped ch-sp), ch 4, 2 sc in next ch-8 lp on current Flower Motif; ch 4, 2 sc in 7th ch-8 lp on 23rd Flower Motif, ch 4, 2 sc in next ch-8 lp on current Flower Motif; ch 8, sc in 6th ch-8 lp on 23rd Flower Motif, ch 3, sc in 5th ch of last ch-8, ch 4; join with sl st in first sc.

EDGING

Sl st in next sc and in next 3 chs of next ch-8 lp, ch 1, 2 sc in same ch-8 lp; *(ch 8, 2 sc in next ch-8 lp on same Flower Motif) 4 times; ch 6, tr tr in ch-3 sp of last joining on Rnd 5 of Flower Motifs, ch 6**; 2 sc in first ch-8 lp on next Flower Motif; rep from * around, ending final rep at **: 240 sc, 24 tr tr, 96 ch-8 lps, and 48 ch-6 lps; join with sl st in first sc. Finish off; weave in ends. Set aside Flower Motif Ring.

CENTER

Ch 6; join with sl st to form a ring.

Rnd 1 (right side): Ch 3 (counts as dc), 23 dc in ring: 24 dc; join with sl st in 3rd ch of beg ch-3.

Rnd 2: Ch 4 (counts as dc and ch-1 sp); *dc in next dc, ch 1; rep from * around: 24 dc and 24 ch-1 sps; join with sl st in 3rd ch of beg ch-4.

Rnd 3: Sl st in first ch-1 sp, ch 6 (counts as tr and ch-2 sp); *tr in next ch-1 sp, ch 2; rep from * around: 24 tr and 24 ch-2 sps; join with sl st in 4th ch of beg ch-6.

Rnd 4: Sl st in first ch-2 sp, ch 7 (counts as tr and ch-3 sp); *tr in next ch-2 sp, ch 3; rep from * around: 24 tr and 24 ch-3 sps; join with sl st in 4th ch of beg ch-7.

Rnd 5: Sl st in first ch-3 sp, ch 4 (counts as tr), 6 tr in same ch-3 sp, ch 5; *skip next ch-3 sp, 7 tr in next ch-3 sp, ch 5; rep from * around: 84 tr and 12 ch-5 lps; join with sl st in 4th ch of beg ch-4.

Rnd 6: Ch 4 (counts as tr), tr in each of next 6 tr, ch 7; *tr in each of next 7 tr, ch 7; rep from * around: 84 tr and 12 ch-7 lps; join as before.

Rnd 7: Work beg 7 dtr dec in next 6 tr; *ch 5, skip next 2 chs, 2 tr in each of next 3 chs, skip next 2 chs, ch 5**; 7 dtr dec in next 7 tr; rep from * around, ending final rep at **: twelve 7 dtr dec, 72 tr and 24 ch-5 lps; join with sl st in top of 6 dtr dec.

Rnd 8: Ch 12, 6 tr dec in next 6 tr, ch 12; *sc in top of next 7 dtr dec, ch 12, 6 tr dec in next 6 tr, ch 12; rep from * around, omitting final ch 12; ch 6, tr tr in joining sl st (counts as ch-12 lp): twelve 6 tr dec, 11 sc and 24 ch-12 lps.

Rnd 9: Ch 1, (sc, ch 3, sc) around post of joining tr tr, ch 12; *(sc, ch 3, sc) in next ch-12 lp, ch 12; rep from * around: 48 sc, 24 ch-3 sps and 24 ch-12 lps; join with sl st in first sc.

Rnd 10: Sl st in next ch-sp and in next sc, sl st in next 5 chs, ch 6 (counts as tr and ch-2 sp), skip next 2 chs, tr in next ch, ch 8; *tr in 5th ch of next ch-12 lp, ch 2, skip next 2 chs, tr in next ch, ch 8; rep from * around: 48 tr, 24 ch-2 sps and 24 ch-8 lps; join with sl st in 4th ch of beg ch-6.

Rnd 11: Sl st in first ch-2 sp, ch 4 (counts as tr), 3 tr in same ch-2 sp, ch 9; *skip next ch-8 lp, 4 tr in next ch-2 sp, ch 9; rep from * around: 96 tr and 24 ch-9 lps; join with sl st in 4th ch of beg ch-4.

Rnd 12: Ch 6 (counts as tr and ch-2 sp), skip next 2 tr, tr in next tr; *ch 5, sc around next ch-9 lp on Rnd 11 and next ch-8 lp on Rnd 10, ch 5**; tr in next tr, ch 2, skip next 2 tr, tr in next tr; rep from * around, ending final rep at **: 48 tr, 24 sc, 24 ch-2 sps and 48 ch-5 lps; join with sl st in 4th ch of beg ch-6.

Rnd 13: Sl st in first ch-2 sp, ch 4 (counts as tr), 4 tr in same ch-2 sp, ch 12; *5 tr in next ch-2 sp, ch 12; rep from * around: 120 tr and 24 ch-12 lps; join with sl st in 4th ch of beg ch-4.

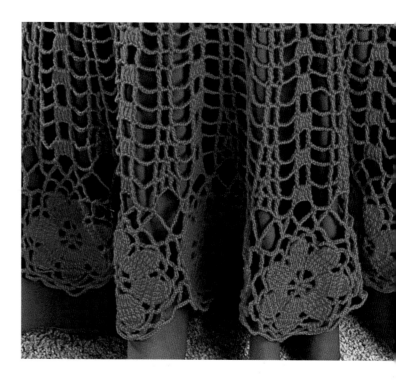

Rnd 14: Ch 6 (counts as tr and ch-2 sp), skip next 3 tr, tr in next tr; *ch 4, tr in 5th ch of next ch-12 lp, ch 2, skip next 2 chs, tr in next ch, ch 4**; tr in next tr, ch 2, skip next 3 tr, tr in next tr; rep from * around, ending final rep at **: 96 tr, 48 ch-4 lps and 48 ch-2 sps; join with sl st in 4th ch of beg ch-6.

Rnd 15: Sl st in first ch-2 sp, ch 4 (counts as tr), 4 tr in same ch-2 sp; *ch 4, tr in next tr, ch 2, tr in next tr, ch 4**; 5 tr in next ch-2 sp; rep from * around, ending final rep at **: 168 tr, 48 ch-4 lps and 24 ch-2 sps; join with sl st in 4th ch of beg ch-4.

Rnd 16: Ch 6 (counts as tr and ch-2 sp), skip next 3 tr, tr in next tr; *ch 4, tr in next tr, ch 2, tr in next tr, ch 4**; tr in next tr, ch 2, skip next 3 tr, tr in next tr; rep from * around, ending final rep at **: 96 tr, 48 ch-4 lps and 48 ch-2 sps; join with sl st in 4th ch of beg ch-6.

Rnd 17: Sl st in first ch-2 sp, ch 4 (counts as tr), 4 tr in same ch-2 sp; *ch 5, tr in next tr, ch 2, tr in next tr, ch 5**; 5 tr in next ch-2 sp; rep from * around, ending final rep at **: 168 tr, 48 ch-5 lps and 24 ch-2 sps; join with sl st in 4th ch of beg ch-4.

Rnd 18: Ch 6 (counts as tr and ch-2 sp), skip next 3 tr, tr in next tr; *ch 5, tr in next tr, ch 2, tr in next tr, ch 5**; tr in next tr, ch 2, skip next 3 tr, tr in next tr; rep from * around, ending final rep at **: 96 tr, 48 ch-5 lps and 48 ch-2 sps; join with sl st in 4th ch of beg ch-6.

Rnds 19 and 20: Rep Rnds 17 and 18.

Rnd 21: Sl st in first ch-2 sp, ch 4 (counts as tr), 4 tr in same ch-2 sp; *ch 7, tr in next tr, ch 2, tr in next tr, ch 7**; 5 tr in next ch-2 sp; rep from * around, ending final rep at **: 168 tr, 48 ch-7 lps and 24 ch-2 sps; join with sl st in 4th ch of beg ch-4.

Rnd 22: Ch 7 (counts as tr and ch-3 sp), skip next 3 tr, tr in next tr; *ch 7, tr in next tr, ch 2, tr in next tr, ch 7**; tr in next tr, ch 3, skip next 3 tr, tr in next tr; rep from * around, ending final rep at **: 96 tr, 48 ch-7 lps, 24 ch-3 sps and 24 ch-2 sps; join with sl st in 4th ch of beg ch-6.

Rnd 23: Ch 4 (counts as tr), 3 tr in next ch-3 sp, tr in next tr; *ch 7, tr in next tr, ch 3, tr in next tr, ch 7**; tr in next tr, 3 tr in next ch-3 sp, tr in next tr; rep from * around, ending final rep at **: 168 tr, 48 ch-7 lps and 24 ch-3 sps; join with sl st in 4th ch of beg ch-4.

Rnd 24: Ch 7 (counts as tr and ch-3 sp), skip next 3 tr, tr in next tr; * ch 7, tr in next tr, ch 2, tr in next ch-3 sp, ch 2, tr in next tr, ch 7**; tr in next tr, ch 3, skip next 3 tr, tr in next tr; rep from * around, ending final rep at **: 120 tr, 48 ch-7 lps, 24 ch-3 sps and 48 ch-2 sps; join with sl st in 4th ch of beg ch-7.

Rnd 25: Ch 4 (counts as tr), 3 tr in next ch-3 sp, tr in next tr; *ch 7, (tr in next tr, ch 2) 2 times, tr in next tr, ch 7**; tr in next tr, 3 tr in next ch-3 sp, tr in next tr; rep from * around, ending final rep at **: 192 tr, 48 ch-7 lps and 48 ch-2 sps; join with sl st in 4th ch of beg ch-4.

Rnd 26: Ch 7 (counts as tr and ch-3 sp), skip next 3 tr, tr in next tr; *ch 7, tr in next tr, ch 2, (tr, ch 2, tr) in next tr, ch 2, tr in next tr, ch 7**; tr in next tr, ch 3, skip next 3 tr, tr in next tr; rep from * around, ending final rep at **: 144 tr, 48 ch-7 lps, 24 ch-3 sps and 72 ch-2 sps; join with sl st in 4th ch of beg ch-7.

Rnd 27: Ch 4 (counts as tr), 3 tr in first ch-3 sp, tr in next tr; *ch 7, (tr in next tr, ch 2) 3 times, tr in next tr**; ch 7, tr in next tr, 3 tr in next ch-3 sp, tr in next tr; rep from * around, ending final rep at **; ch 3, join with tr in 4th ch of beg ch-4 (counts as ch-7 lp): 216 tr, 48 ch-7 lps and 72 ch-2 sps.

Note: *Center is joined to Flower Motif Ring with right sides facing.*

Rnd 28 (joining rnd): Ch 1, sc around post of joining tr; *ch 5, sc in 10th ch-8 lp on adjacent Flower Motif, ch 5, sc in next ch-7 lp of Center; ch 5, sc in 9th ch-8 lp on same adjacent Flower Motif, ch 5, sc in same ch-7 lp of Center; ch 7, sc in marked ch-sp between same adjacent Flower Motif and next adjacent Flower Motif, ch 7, skip next 3 ch-2 sps on Center; sc in next ch-7 lp of Center; ch 5, sc in 11th ch-8 lp on next adjacent Flower Motif, ch 5**; sc in same ch-7 lp of Center; rep from * around, ending final rep at **; join with sl st in first sc. Finish off; weave in ends.

Daisy Filigree Tablecloth

Dainty daisy motifs are joined to form this charming cloth, and are joined as you go. The result is a lacy cloth that will suit any décor.

SIZE: 77" x 92"

MATERIALS

Size 10 (bedspread weight) crochet thread
25 balls (400 yds each) or 10,000 yds white
Size 7 (1.65 mm) steel crochet hook
   (or size required for gauge)

GAUGE

Motif = 2^1/2" square

SPECIAL STITCHES

3 double triple cluster (3 dtr cl): YO 3 times, insert hook in first specified st and draw up a lp, (YO and draw through 2 lps on hook) 3 times; *YO 3 times, insert hook in 2nd specified st and draw up a lp, (YO and draw through 2 lps on hook) 3 times; rep from * once; YO and draw through all 4 lps on hook: 3 dtr cl made.

4 double triple cluster (4 dtr cl): *YO 3 times, insert hook in first specified st and draw up a lp, (YO and draw through 2 lps on hook) 3 times; rep from * once; **YO 3 times, insert hook in 2nd specified st and draw up a lp, (YO and draw through 2 lps on hook) 3 times; rep from ** once; YO and draw through all 5 lps on hook: 4 dtr cl made.

First Motif

Instructions

FIRST MOTIF

Ch 5; join with sl st to form a ring.

Rnd 1 (right side): Ch 3 (counts as dc), 15 dc in ring: 16 dc; join with sl st in 3rd ch of beg ch-3.

Rnd 2: Ch 5, 3 dtr cl in same ch as joining and in next dc; *ch 8, 4 dtr cl in next 2 dc; rep from * 6 times more; ch 8: 8 dtr cl and 8 ch-8 sps; join with sl st in top of 3 dtr cl.

Rnd 3: Ch 1; *6 sc in next ch-8 sp, ch 7, 6 sc in same ch-8 sp, 12 sc in next ch-8 sp; rep from * 3 times more: 96 sc and 4 ch-7 sps; join with sl st in beg sc. Finish off; weave in ends.

Note: *Join motifs with right sides facing into 29 rows of 35 motifs each working a corner motif in each of 4 corners.*

MOTIF WITH ONE SIDE JOINING

Rnds 1 and 2: Rep Rnds 1 and 2 on First Motif.

Rnd 3: Ch 1; *6 sc in next ch-8 sp, ch 7, 6 sc in same ch-8 sp, 12 sc in next ch-8 sp; rep from * once more; **6 sc in next ch-8 sp, ch 3, join with sc in 4th ch of ch-7 on adjacent motif, ch 3, 6 sc in same ch-8 sp on current motif**; 6 sc in next ch-8 sp, join with sc in 7th sc of 12 sc on same adjacent motif, 6 sc in same ch-8 sp on current motif; rep from ** to ** once; 12 sc in next ch-8 sp: 96 sc, 2 ch-7 sps and 3 joinings; join with sl st in beg sc. Finish off; weave in ends.

MOTIF WITH TWO SIDE JOINING

Rnds 1 and 2: Rep Rnds 1 and 2 on First Motif.

Rnd 3: Ch 1, 6 sc in next ch-8 sp, ch 7, 6 sc in same ch-8 sp, 12 sc in next ch-8 sp; *6 sc in next ch-8 sp, ch 3, join with sc in 4th ch of ch-7 on first adjacent motif, ch 3, 6 sc in same ch-8 sp on current motif**; 6 sc in next ch-8 sp, join with sc in 7th sc of 12 sc on same adjacent motif, 6 sc in same ch-8 sp on current motif; rep from * once, working first joining sc in previous joining of 2 adjacent motifs and second joining sc on second adjacent motif; rep from * to ** once, working joining sc on second adjacent motif; 12 sc in next ch-8 sp: 96 sc, one ch-7 sp and 5 joinings; join with sl st in beg sc. Finish off; weave in ends.

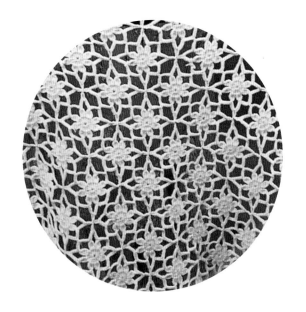

CORNER MOTIF

(make 4)

Rnds 1 and 2: Rep Rnds 1 and 2 on First Motif.

Rnd 3: Ch 1, 6 sc in next ch-8 sp, ch 7, sc in same ch-8 sp, ch 7, 6 sc in same ch-8 sp, 12 sc in next ch-8 sp; *6 sc in next ch-8 sp, ch 3, join with sc in 4th ch of ch-7 on first adjacent motif, ch 3, 6 sc in same ch-8 sp on current motif**; 6 sc in next ch-8 sp, join with sc in 7th sc of 12 sc on same adjacent motif, 6 sc in same ch-8 sp on current motif; rep from * once, working first joining sc in previous joining of 2 adjacent motifs and second joining sc on second adjacent motif; rep from * to ** once, working joining sc on second adjacent motif; 12 sc in next ch-8 sp: 96 sc, two ch-7 sps and 5 joinings; join with sl st in beg sc. Finish off; weave in ends.

EDGING

Rnd 1: With right side facing, join with sc in 4th ch of first ch-7 sp on any corner motif; **ch 5, sc in 4th ch of next ch-7 sp on same motif, ch 11, sc in 7th sc of 12 sc on side of same motif; *ch 11, sc in motif joining, ch 11, sc in 7th sc of 12 sc on side of next motif; rep from * to next corner; ch 11***; sc in 4th ch of first ch-7 sp on next corner motif; rep from ** 2 times more; rep from ** to *** once: 4 corner ch-5 sps and 256 ch-11 sps; join with sl st in beg sc.

Rnd 2: Ch 1; **7 sc in corner ch-5 sp; *15 sc in next ch-11 sp; rep from * to next corner; rep from ** around; join as before.

Rnd 3: Ch 5; **(dc, ch 7, dc) in 4th sc of 7 sc in corner, ch 2, dc in first sc of next 15 sc; *ch 2, skip next 2 sc, dc in next sc; rep from * 3 times more; rep from ** across to next corner; ch 2***; dc in first sc of 7 sc in next corner, ch 2; rep from ** two times more; rep from ** to *** once; join with sl st in 3rd ch of beg ch-5.

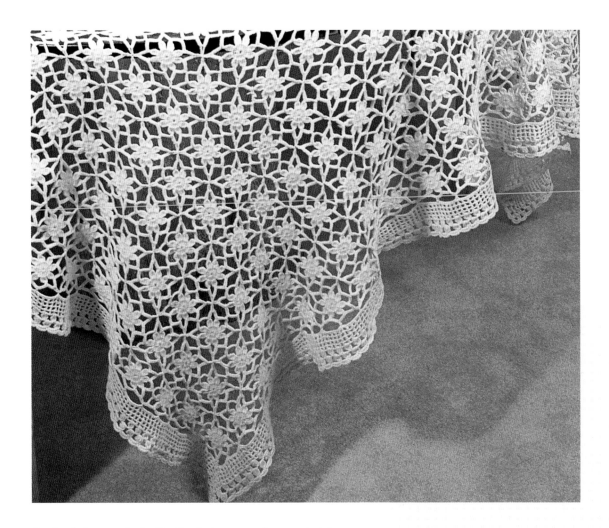

Rnds 4 through 6: Ch 5, dc in next dc; work (ch 2, dc, ch 7, dc) in 4th ch of each corner ch-7 sp and (ch 2, dc) in each dc around; ch 2; join as before.

Rnd 7: Sl st in next ch-2 sp, ch 5, 3 dtr cl in same ch-2 sp, ch 5, skip next ch-2 sp, 4 dtr cl in next ch-2 sp; **ch 5, skip next ch-2 sp, (4 dtr cl, ch 7, 4 dtr cl) in corner ch-7 sp; *ch 5, skip next ch-2 sp, 4 dtr cl in next ch-2 sp; rep from * across to next corner; rep from ** around to beg; ch 5; join with sl st in top of beg 3 dtr cl.

Rnd 8: Sl st in next ch and in ch-5 sp, ch 5, 3 dtr cl in same ch-5 sp; *ch 5, 4 dtr cl in next ch-5 sp; **ch 5, (4 dtr cl, ch 7, 4 dtr cl) in corner ch-7 sp; ***ch 5, 4 dtr cl in next ch-5 sp; rep from *** to next corner ch-7 sp; rep from ** around to beg; ch 5; join as before.

Rnd 9: *Ch 1, 5 dc in next ch-5 sp, sc in top of next dtr cl**; rep from * across to next corner; ch 1, 7 dc in corner ch-7 sp, sc in top of next dtr cl; rep from * two times more; rep from * to ** across to beg; join with sl st in joining sl st. Finish off; weave in ends.

Harvest Cloth

This unusual cloth has an interesting history. European in origin, the family which inherited it told us that it was used at harvest time to cover offerings of produce given to the local church. The unusual filet symbols—animals, an angel, a church, a home—lend credence to the idea, although we do not know their meanings.

SIZE: 25" x 28" plus 6" border

MATERIALS
Size 20 crochet cotton,
    13 balls (400 yds each) or 5,200 yds white
Size 11 (1.10 mm) steel crochet hook
    (or size required for gauge)
Stitch markers
Straight pins

GAUGE
19 mesh = 4"; 20 mesh rows = 4"

Instructions

Note: *Charts vary slightly from photo to ensure uniformity.*

CENTER

Note: *Center is worked from side to side instead of from bottom to top. Chart is made to reflect direction of work. Start at bottom of chart and work up toward top of chart.*

Ch 402.

Row 1 (right side): Dc in 9th ch from hook, dc in next 3 chs; *ch 2, skip 2 chs, dc in next 4 chs; rep from * across: 66 open mesh and 66 closed mesh; ch 5, turn.

Rows 2 through 126: Work open and closed mesh as per chart and filet instructions on pages 134-138. At end of Row 126, finish off; weave in ends.

BORDER

Ch 75.

Row 1 (right side): Dc in 9th ch from hook, dc in next 3 chs; ch 2, skip 2 chs, dc in next 4 chs; *ch 2, skip 2 chs, dc in next ch; rep from * 16 times more; dc in next 3 chs, ch 2, skip 2 chs, dc in last ch: 20 open mesh and 3 closed mesh; ch 5, turn.

Rows 2 through 56: Work open mesh, closed mesh, inc and dec as per chart and filet instructions on pages 134-138.

Rep Rows 29 through 56 on chart until border measures about 132" long, ending by working a Row 56 rep. At end of last row, finish off; weave in ends.

FINISHING

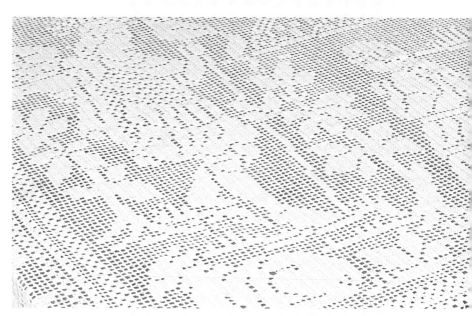

Being careful not to twist Border, whip stitch first and last rows of Border together. Fold Border in half twice and place marker in each fold to mark four equal parts of Border. Fold Center in half each way and place marker in middle of each edge. With right sides and straight edges facing, pin each marked spot on Border to each marked spot on Center. Pin remainder of Border to Center, easing in fullness on Border at corners of Center. Whip stitch straight edge of border to edges of center.

EDGING

With right side facing, join with sc in last ch-sp at edge of last row of Border; *ch 5, sc in top of last sc made; (dc, ch 5, sc in top of last dc made) 3 times in next ch-sp; sc in next ch-sp; rep from * around entire edge of Border; join with sl st in beg sc. Finish off; weave in ends.

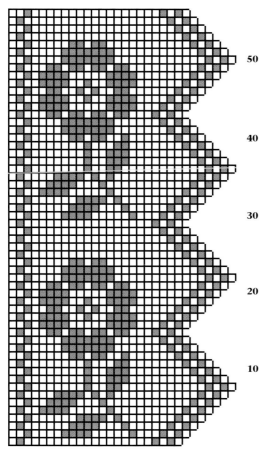

Border

KEY

□ open mesh

■ closed mesh

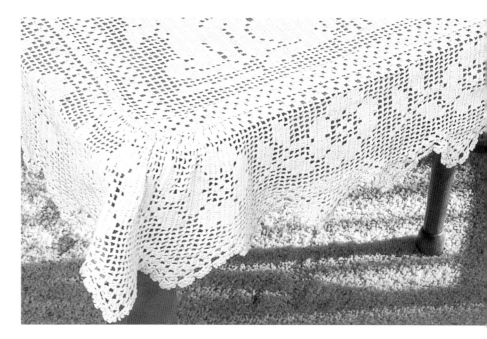

harvest cloth

Center—Left

KEY
- □ open mesh
- ■ closed mesh

94

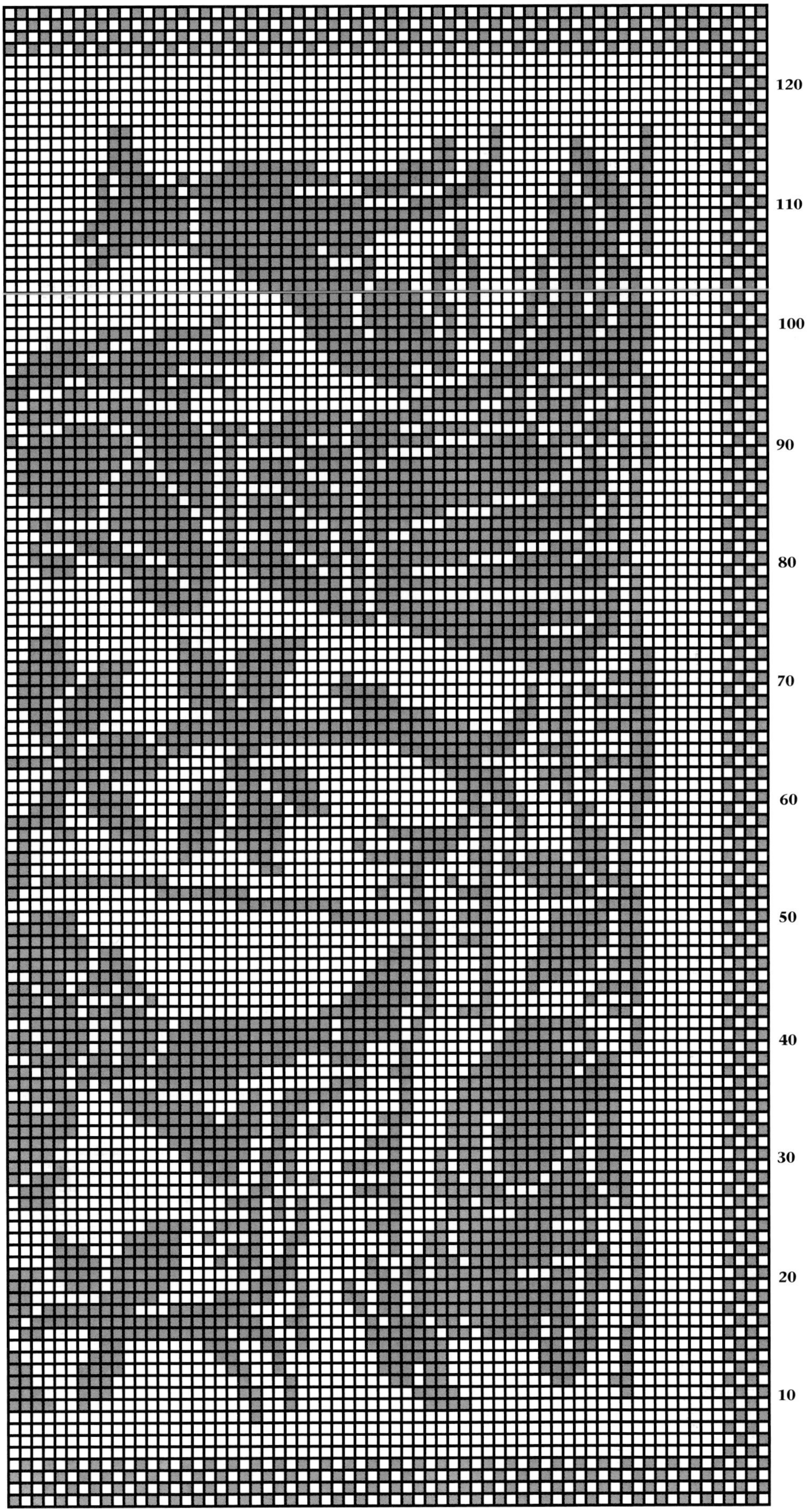
120
110
100
90
80
70
60
50
40
30
20
10

Center—Right

Frosty Pineapples Bedspread

Pineapple squares worked in a frosty white thread make this a striking bedspread. A pretty edging is worked on all four sides.

SIZE: 66" x 114"

MATERIALS

Size 10 (bedspread weight) crochet thread
   31 balls (400 yds each) or 12,400 yds white
Size 5 (1.90 mm) steel crochet hook
   (or size required for gauge)
Stitch markers

GAUGE

Motif Rnds 1 and 2 = 2 1/8" diameter;
Full motif = 6" square

SPECIAL STITCHES

Beg 3 triple cluster (beg 3 tr CL): Ch 4; *YO twice, insert hook in specified st or sp and draw up a lp, (YO and draw through 2 lps on hook) twice; rep from * once more; YO and draw through all 3 lps on hook: beg 3 tr CL made.

3 triple cluster (3 tr CL): *YO twice, insert hook in specified st or sp and draw up a lp, (YO and draw through 2 lps on hook) twice; rep from * 2 times more; YO and draw through all 4 lps on hook: 3 tr CL made.

6 dc cluster (6 dc CL): YO, insert hook in first specified st and draw up a lp, YO and draw through 2 lps on hook; *YO, insert hook in next specified st and draw up a lp, YO and draw through 2 lps on hook; rep from * 4 times more; YO and draw through all 7 lps on hook: 6 dc CL made.

V-stitch (V-st): Work (dc, ch 2, dc) in specified st or sp: V-st made.

V-st in next V-st: Work V-st in ch-2 sp of next V-st.

Picot: Ch 3, sc in top of last sc: picot made.

Instructions

MOTIF

(make 180)

Ch 10; join with sl st to form a ring.

Rnd 1 (right side): Work beg 3 tr CL in ring, ch 4; *3 tr CL in ring, ch 4; rep from * 6 times more: eight 3 tr CL and 8 ch-4 lps; join with sl st in top of beg 3 tr CL.

Rnd 2: Sl st in next 2 chs, ch 3 (counts as dc now and throughout), 2 dc in same ch-4 lp; *ch 4, 5 tr in next ch-4 lp, ch 4**; 3 dc in next ch-4 lp; rep from * 3 times more, ending final rep at **: 20 tr, 12 dc and 8 ch-4 lps; join with sl st in 3rd ch of beg ch-3.

Rnd 3: Ch 3, dc in same ch as joining; *(dc, ch 2, dc) in next dc, 2 dc in next dc, ch 4, sc in next 5 tr, ch 4**; 2 dc in next dc; rep from * 3 times more, ending final rep at **: 24 dc, 20 sc, 8 ch-4 lps and 4 ch-2 sps; join as before.

Rnd 4: Ch 3, dc in next 2 dc; *(dc, ch 2, dc) in next ch-2 sp, dc in next 3 dc, ch 4, sc in next 5 sc, ch 4**; dc in next 3 dc; rep from * 3 times more, ending final rep at **: 32 dc, 20 sc, 8 ch-4 lps and 4 ch-2 sps; join.

Rnd 5: Ch 3, dc in next 2 dc; *ch 2, skip next dc, (dc, ch 2) 4 times in next ch-2 sp, skip next dc, dc in next 3 dc, ch 4, sc in next sc, (ch 3, sc in next sc) 4 times, ch 4**; dc in next 3 dc; rep from * 3 times more, ending final rep at **: 40 dc, 20 sc, 8 ch-4 ls, 16 ch-3 sps and 20 ch-2 sps; join.

Rnd 6: Ch 3, dc in next 2 dc; *(ch 2, dc in next ch-2 sp) 2 times, ch 2, (dc, ch 2, dc) in next ch-2 sp, (ch 2, dc in next ch-2 sp) 2 times, ch 2, dc in next 3 dc, ch 4, sc in next ch-3 sp, (ch 3, sc in next ch-3 sp) 3 times, ch 4**; dc in next 3 dc; rep from * 3 times more, ending final rep at **: 48 dc, 16 sc, 8 ch-4 lps, 12 ch-3 sps and 28 ch-2 sps; join.

Rnd 7: Ch 3, dc in next 2 dc; *(ch 2, dc in next ch-2 sp) 3 times, ch 2, 4 dc in next ch-2 sp, (ch 2, dc in next ch-2 sp) 3 times, ch 2, dc in next 3 dc, ch 4, sc in next ch-3 sp, (ch 3, sc in next ch-3 sp) 2 times, ch 4**; dc in next 3 dc; rep from * 3 times more, ending final rep at **: 64 dc, 12 sc, 8 ch-4 lps, 8 ch-3 sps and 32 ch-2 sps; join.

Rnd 8: Ch 3, dc in next 2 dc; *(ch 2, dc in next ch-2 sp) 4 times, ch 5, (dc in next ch-2 sp, ch 2) 4 times, dc in next 3 dc, ch 4, sc in next ch-3 sp, ch 3, sc in next ch-3 sp, ch 4**; dc in next 3 dc; rep from * 3 times more, ending final rep at **: 56 dc, 8 sc, 4 ch-5 lps, 8 ch-4 lps, 4 ch-3 sps and 32 ch-2 sps; join.

Rnd 9: Ch 3, dc in next 2 dc; *(ch 2, dc in next ch-2 sp) 4 times, (ch 2, 3 tr CL) 4 times in next ch-5 lp, (ch 2, dc in next ch-2 sp) 4 times, ch 2, dc in next 3 dc, ch 4, sc in next ch-3 sp, ch 4**; dc in next 3 dc; rep from * 3 times more, ending final rep at **: sixteen 3 tr CL, 56 dc, 4 sc, 8 ch-4 lps and 52 ch-2 sps; join.

Rnd 10: Sl st in next 2 dc, sl st in next ch-2 sp and in next dc, ch 3; *2 dc in next ch-2 sp, dc in next dc, ch 2, dc in next dc, 2 dc in next ch-2 sp, dc in next dc, ch 2**; dc in top of next 3 tr CL, ch 2, skip next ch-2 sp, (tr, ch 1) 4 times in next ch-2 sp, tr in same ch-2 sp, ch 2, skip next ch-2 sp, dc in top of next 3 tr CL, ch 2, dc in next dc; rep from * to ** once; 6 dc CL in next 6 dc, ch 2**; dc in next dc; rep from * 3 times more, ending final rep at **: four 6 dc CL, 20 tr, 72 dc, 32 ch-2 sps and 16 ch-1 sps; join.

Rnd 11: Ch 1, sc in same ch as joining; sc in each dc, tr, ch-1 sp and 6 dc CL, work 2 sc in each ch-2 sp, work 3 sc in 3rd tr of 5 tr in each corner around: 184 sc; join with sl st in first sc. Finish off; weave in ends.

With right sides facing, whip stitch motifs together into 10 rows of 18 motifs each.

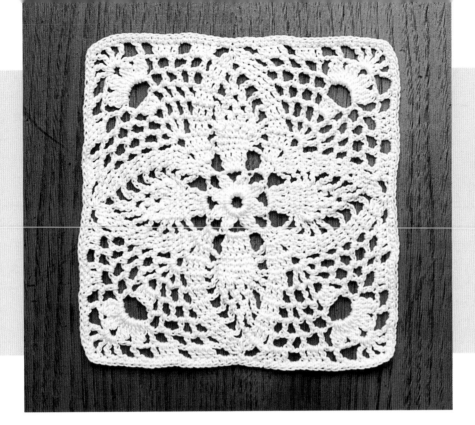

Motif

EDGING

Rnd 1: With right side facing, join with sl st in 2nd sc of 3 sc in any corner, ch 1, 2 sc in same st as joining, work 797 sc evenly along long edges, 442 sc evenly along short edges and 3 sc in center sc of each of other 3 corners, sc in same st as joining (completes 3 sc in first corner): 2490 sc; join with sl st in first sc.

Rnd 2: Ch 7 (counts as dc and ch-4 sp), dc in same st as joining; *ch 2, skip next 2 sc, dc in next sc; rep from * across to next corner; ch 2**; work (dc, ch 4, dc) in center sc of 3 sc in corner; rep from * 3 times more, ending final rep at **: 830 ch-2 sps and 4 corner ch-4 sps; join with sl st in 3rd ch of beg ch-7.

Rnd 3: Sl st in first ch of corner ch-4 sp, ch 8 (counts as dc and ch-5 sp), dc in same corner ch-4 sp; *ch 2, dc in next ch-2 sp; rep from * across to next corner ch-4 sp; ch 2**; work (dc, ch 5, dc) in ch-4 sp of next corner; rep from * 3 times more, ending final rep at **: 834 ch-2 sps and 4 corner ch-5 sps; join with sl st in 3rd ch of beg ch-8.

Rnd 4: Ch 5 (counts as dc and ch-2 sp); *work (dc, ch 4, dc) in ch-5 sp of next corner, ch 2, dc in next dc; **ch 2, dc in next ch-2 sp; rep from ** across to next corner ch-5 sp; ch 2***; dc in next dc, ch 2; rep from * 3 times more, ending final rep at ***: 842 ch-2 sps and 4 corner ch-4 sps; join with sl st in 3rd ch of beg ch-5.

Rnd 5: Sl st in next 2 chs and in next dc, ch 5 (counts as dc and ch-2 sp); *work (dc, ch 4, dc) in ch-4 sp of next corner, ch 2, dc in next dc (place marker in this dc); **ch 2, dc in next ch-2 sp; rep from ** across to next corner ch-4 sp; ch 2***; dc in next dc, ch 2; rep from * 3 times more, ending final rep at ***: 850 ch-2 sps and 4 corner ch-4 sps; join with sl st in 3rd ch of beg ch-5. Finish off; weave in ends.

Rnd 6: With right side facing, join with sl st in any marked st, ch 3 (counts as dc now and through-out); *(2 dc in next ch-2 sp, dc in next dc) 3 times; dc in next ch-2 sp, dc in next dc; ch 2, skip next ch-2 sp**; V-st in next ch-2 sp, ch 2, skip next ch-2 sp; dc in next dc; rep from * across to next corner, ending final rep at **; work (dc, ch 2) 3 times in ch-4 sp of next corner***; skip next dc, dc in next dc; rep from * 3 times more, ending final rep at ***: 1476 dc, 122 V-sts and 260 ch-2 sps; join with sl st in 3rd ch of beg ch-3.

Rnd 7: Sl st in next dc, ch 3, dc in next 9 dc; *ch 2, skip next ch-2 sp, V-st in next V-st, ch 2, skip next ch-2 sp and next dc, dc in next 10 dc; rep from * across to next corner; ch 3, skip next ch-2 sp, V-st in next ch-2 sp, ch 2, V-st in next ch-2 sp, ch 3**; skip next ch-2 sp and next dc, dc in next 10 dc; rep from * 3 times more, ending final rep at **: 1220 dc, 126 V-sts, 8 ch-3 sps and 248 ch-2 sps; join as before.

Rnd 8: Sl st in next dc, ch 3, dc in next 7 dc; *ch 3, skip next ch-2 sp, V-st in next V-st, ch 3, skip next ch-2 sp and next dc, dc in next 8 dc; rep from * across to next corner; ch 3, skip next ch-3 sp, V-st in next V-st, (ch 2, dc) 3 times in next ch-2 sp, ch 2, V-st in next V-st, ch 3**; skip next ch-3 sp and next dc, dc in next 8 dc; rep from * 3 times more, ending final rep at **: 988 dc, 126 V-sts, 244 ch-3 sps and 16 ch-2 sps; join.

Rnd 9: Sl st in next dc, ch 3, dc in next 5 dc; *ch 3, skip next ch-3 sp, (dc, ch 2, dc, ch 2, dc) in ch-2 sp of next V-st, ch 3, skip next ch-3 sp and next dc, dc in next 6 dc; rep from * across to next corner; ch 3, skip next ch-3 sp, V-st in next V-st, ch 2, skip next ch-2 sp, (V-st in next ch-2 sp, ch 2) 2 times, skip next ch-2 sp, V-st in next V-st, ch 3**; skip next ch-3 sp and next dc, dc in next 6 dc; rep from * 3 times more, ending final rep at **: 1086 dc, 16 V-sts, 244 ch-3 sps and 232 ch-2 sps; join.

Rnd 10: Sl st in next dc, ch 3, dc in next 3 dc; *ch 3, skip next ch-3 sp, V-st in next V-st, ch 2, V-st in next V-st, ch 3, skip next ch-3 sp and next dc, dc

in next 4 dc; rep from * across to next corner; ch 3, skip next ch-3 sp, (V-st in next V-st, ch 2, V-st in next ch-2 sp, ch 2) 3 times, V-st in next V-st, ch 3**; skip next ch-3 sp and next dc, dc in next 4 dc; rep from * 3 times more, ending final rep at **: 488 dc, 272 V-sts, 244 ch-3 sps and 146 ch-2 sps; join.

Rnd 11: Sl st in next dc, ch 3, dc in next dc; *ch 3, skip next ch-3 sp, V-st in next V-st, ch 2, V-st in next ch-2 sp, ch 2, V-st in next V-st, ch 3, skip next ch-3 sp and next dc, dc in next 2 dc; rep from * across to next corner; ch 3, skip next ch-3 sp, (V-st in next V-st, ch 2) 3 times, (V-st in next ch-2 sp, ch 2, V-st in next V-st, ch 2) 2 times, V-st in next V-st, ch 2, V-st in next V-st, ch 3**; skip next ch-3 sp and next dc, dc in next 2 dc; rep from * 3 times more, ending final rep at **: 244 dc, 390 V-sts, 244 ch-3 sps and 268 ch-2 sps; join.

Rnd 12: (Sl st, ch 1, sc) in sp before next dc; *(ch 2, V-st in next V-st) 3 times; ch 2, sc in sp between next 2 dc; rep from * across to next corner; (ch 2, V-st in next V-st) 9 times; ch 2**; sc in sp between next 2 dc; rep from * 3 times more, ending final rep at **: 390 V-sts and 512 ch-2 sps; join with sl st in first sc.

Rnd 13: Ch 1, sc in same st as joining; *2 sc in next ch-2 sp, [(sc, picot, sc) in next V-st, (sc, picot, sc) in next ch-2 sp] 2 times, (sc, picot, sc) in next V-st; 2 sc in next ch-2 sp, sc in next sc; rep from * across to next corner; 2 sc in next ch-2 sp, [(sc, picot, sc) in next V-st, (sc, picot, sc) in next ch-2 sp] 8 times; (sc, picot, sc) in next V-st, 2 sc in next ch-2 sp**; sc in next sc; rep from * 3 times more, ending final rep at **: 1926 sc and 678 picots; join as before. Finish off; weave in ends.

Floral Medallions Tablecloth

The rows of floral medallion that make up this cloth are worked in one piece, forming a sweetly simple accent for your dining room.

SIZE: 62" x 69"

MATERIALS
Size 10 crochet cotton,
   25 balls (400 yds each) or 10,000 yds white
Size 8 (1.50 mm) steel crochet hook
   (or size required for gauge)

GAUGE
14 mesh = 4"; 15 mesh rows = 4"

STITCH GUIDE
Picot: Ch 3, sc in top of last dc: picot made.

Shell: Work (3 dc, picot, 3 dc) in specified st or sp: shell made.

Note: *Chart is repeated 6 times across tablecloth. First open mesh in each row is worked as beg open mesh. Last open mesh in each row is worked as end open mesh.*

Instructions

Ch 654.

Row 1 (right side): Dc in 9th ch from hook; *ch 2, skip 2 chs, dc in next ch; rep from * across: 216 open mesh; ch 5, turn.

Rows 2 through 7: Work open and closed mesh as per chart and filet instructions on pages 134-138.

Row 8: *[Work 2 open mesh, 4 closed mesh, 1 open mesh, 1 closed mesh, ch 3, skip next closed mesh, sc in ch-2 sp of next open mesh, ch 3, skip next closed mesh, 1 closed mesh, 1 open mesh, 4 closed mesh] 2 times; 2 open mesh; rep from * 5 times more: 120 closed mesh, 60 open mesh, 24 ch-3 sps and 12 sc; ch 5, turn.

Row 9: *Work 3 open mesh; **2 closed mesh, 1 open mesh, 1 closed mesh, ch 3, skip next closed mesh, [sc in next ch-3 sp, ch 3] 2 times, skip next closed mesh, 1 closed mesh, 1 open mesh, 2 closed mesh**; 4 open mesh; rep from ** to ** once; 3 open mesh; rep from * 5 times more: 72 closed mesh, 84 open mesh, 36 ch-3 sps and 24 sc; ch 5, turn.

Row 10: *Work 5 open mesh; **1 closed mesh, ch 3, skip next closed mesh, [sc in next ch-3 sp, ch 3] 3 times, skip next closed mesh, 1 closed mesh**; 8 open mesh; rep from ** to ** once; 5 open mesh; rep from * 5 times more: 24 closed mesh, 108 open mesh, 48 ch-3 sps and 36 sc; ch 5, turn.

Row 11: *Work 3 open mesh; **2 closed mesh, 1 open mesh, 3 dc in next ch-3 sp (closed mesh made); ch 3, [sc in next ch-3 sp, ch 3] 2 times; 3 dc in next ch-3 sp, dc in next dc (closed mesh made); 1 open mesh, 2 closed mesh**; 4 open mesh; rep from ** to ** once; 3 open mesh; rep from * 5 times more: 72 closed mesh, 84 open mesh, 36 ch-3 sps and 24 sc; ch 5, turn.

Row 12: *[Work 2 open mesh, 4 closed mesh, 1 open mesh, 3 dc in next ch-3 sp (closed mesh made), ch 3, sc in next ch-3 sp, ch 3; 3 dc in next ch-3 sp, dc in next dc (closed mesh made); 1 open mesh, 4 closed mesh] 2 times; 2 open mesh; rep from * 5 times more: 120 closed mesh, 60 open mesh, 24 ch-3 sps and 12 sc; ch 5, turn.

Row 13: *[Work 2 open mesh, 4 closed mesh, 2 open mesh; 3 dc in next ch-3 sp (closed mesh made); ch 2, 3 dc in next ch-3 sp, dc in next dc (1 open and 1 closed mesh made); 2 open mesh, 4 closed mesh] 2 times; 2 open mesh; rep from * 5 times more: 120 closed mesh and 96 open mesh; ch 5, turn.

Rows 14 through 19: Work open and closed mesh as per chart and filet instructions on pages 134-138.

Rep Rows 3 through 19 fourteen times more. At end of last row, finish off; weave in ends.

EDGING

With right side facing, join with sl st in 3rd ch of turning ch-5 in top right-hand corner, ch 1, sc in same ch as joining; *ch 3, skip next ch-2 sp, shell in next ch-2 sp, ch 3, skip next ch-2 sp, sc in next ch-2 sp; rep from * 52 times more across; ch 3, skip next ch-2 sp, shell in next ch-2 sp, ch 4, skip next 2 ch-2 sps, sc in corner dc or ch; ch 4, skip edge of next 2 rows, shell in edge of next row, ch 3, skip edge of next row, sc in edge of next row; **ch 3, skip edge of next row, shell in edge of next row, ch 3, skip edge of next row, sc in edge of next row; rep from ** 61 times more across edge of rows; ch 3, skip edge of next row, shell in edge of next row, ch 4, skip edge of next 2 rows, sc in corner ch; rep from * around to beg corner, omitting final sc: 236 shells; join with sl st in beg sc. Finish off; weave in ends.

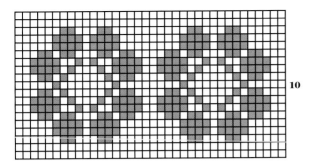

Chart

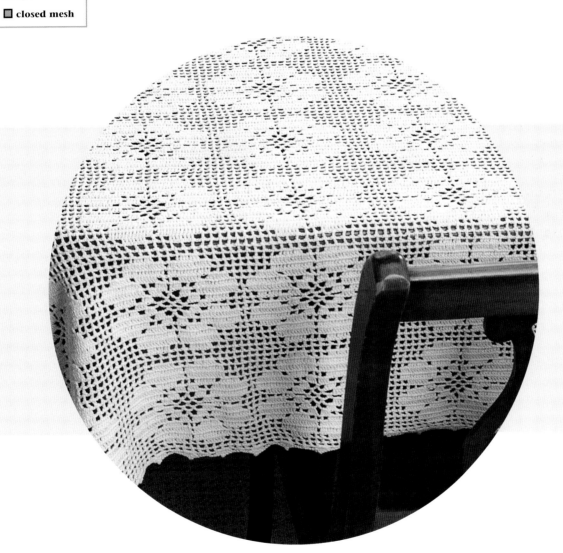

Adjustable Size Pineapple Tablecloth

The square pineapple blocks let you do a bit of math to change the size to fit any table, or even to create a bedspread.

SIZE: Adjustable to any desired size.

To determine size: *Measure the length and width of your table, then add 20" to each dimension to allow 10" on each side for the overhang. For example, if your table is 45" by 55", add 20" to each for a total of 65" x 75". Each square when worked to gauge measures 5½". So divide 65" by 5½" and you will need (rounded off) 12 squares for the width. Now divide the 75" length by 5½ and you will need 13 squares for the length. Multiply these two numbers (12 and 13) and the result is 156 squares.*

MATERIALS

Size 10 crochet cotton

To determine amount of crochet thread needed: *Since each square requires 50 yds of thread, multiply the total number of squares needed by 50 yds. In the example above, this would mean 7,800 yds. Check the yardage on the brand of thread you are using to determine the amount needed. If each ball of thread has 350 yds,then divide 350 into 7,800 and you will need 23 balls. Be sure to buy all of the yarn you need from the same dye lot.*

50 yds for each square needed (see above)

Size 6 (1.8 mm) steel crochet hook

(or size required for gauge.)

GAUGE

Rnds 1 through 3 of Square = 1¾"
Completed 13-rnd Square = 5½" x 5½"

SPECIAL STITCHES

Cluster (CL): (YO 2 times; insert hook in specified st or sp and draw up a lp; YO and draw through first 2 lps on hook twice) 3 times; YO and draw through all 4 lps on hook: CL made.

Instructions

FIRST SQUARE

Note: *All rnds are worked from the right side; do not turn.*

Ch 12, join with sl st to form a ring.

Rnd l: Ch 3, 31 dc in ring: 32 dc made, counting beg ch-3 as a dc; sl st in top of beg ch-3.

Rnd 2: Ch 1, sc in joining; (ch 12, skip 7 dc, sc in next dc) 3 times; ch 12, skip 7 dc; sl st in beg sc.

Rnd 3: Sl st in next ch-12 sp, ch 4 (counts as a tr), 9 tr in next ch-12 sp, ch 5; (10 tr in next ch-12 sp, ch 5) 3 times; sl st in 4th ch of beg ch-4. **Note:** *Each 10-tr group forms the base of a pineapple.*

Rnd 4: Ch 5, (tr in next tr, ch 1) 8 times, tr in next tr; * [ch 3, sc in next ch-5 sp, ch 3; (tr in next tr, ch 1) 9 times, tr in next tr;] 3 times; ch 3, sc in next ch-5 sp, ch 3, sl st in top ch of beg ch-4.

Rnd 5: Sl st in next ch-1 sp, in next tr work (sl st, ch 1, sc); ch 3, sc in next tr; * † (ch 3, sc in next tr) 7 times, ch 5; skip next ch-3 sp, next sc, next

ch-3 sp, next tr, and next ch-1 sp †; (sc, ch 3, sc) in next tr; rep from * 2 times more, then rep from † to † one time; sl st in beg sc.

Rnd 6: In next ch-3 sp work (sl st, ch 1, sc) * †; (ch 3, sc in next ch-3 sp) 7 times; ch 3, 3 dc in next ch-5 sp; ch 3 †, sc in next ch-3 sp; rep from * two times more; rep from † to † once, sl st in beg sc.

Rnd 7: In next ch-3 sp work (sl st, ch 1, sc); * † (ch 3, sc in next ch-3 sp) 6 times; ch 3, 3 dc in next ch-3 sp, ch 7, 3 dc in next ch-3 sp, ch 3 †; sc in next ch-3 sp; rep from * twice more, then rep from †to †once; sl st in beg sc.

Rnd 8: In next ch-3 sp work (sl st, ch 1, sc); * † (ch 3, sc in next ch-3 sp) 5 times; ch 3, 3 dc in next ch-3 sp, ch 7, sc in next ch-7 sp, ch 7, 3 dc in next ch-3 sp, ch 3 †; sc in next ch-3 sp; rep from * two times more, then rep from † to † one more time; sl st in beg sc.

Rnd 9: In next ch-3 sp work (sl st, ch 1, sc); * † (ch 3, sc in next ch-3 sp) 4 times; ch 3, 3 dc in next ch-3 sp; (ch 7, sc in next ch-7 sp) two times; ch 7, 3 dc in next ch-3 sp, ch 3 †; sc in next ch-3 sp; rep from * two times more, then rep from † to † one time; sl st in beg sc.

Rnd 10: In next ch-3 sp work (sl st, ch 1, sc); * † (ch 3, sc in next ch-3 sp) 3 times; ch 3, 3 dc in next ch-3 sp, ch 5, sc in next ch-7 sp, ch 5, in next ch-7 sp work (CL, ch 5) 3 times; sc in next ch-7 sp, ch 5, 3 dc in next ch-3 sp; ch 3 †; sc in next ch-3 sp; rep from * two times more, then rep from † to † one time; sl st in beg sc.

Rnd 11: In next ch-3 sp work (sl st, ch 1, sc); * †(ch 3, sc in next ch-3 sp) twice; ch 3, 3 dc in next ch-3 sp, (ch 7, sc in next ch-5 sp) twice; ch 5, sc in next ch-5 sp, ch 12, sc in next ch-5 sp, ch 5, sc in next ch-5 sp, ch 7, sc in next ch-5 sp, ch 7; 3 dc in next ch-3 sp, ch 3 †; sc in next ch-3 sp; rep from * two more times, then rep from † to † one more time; sl st in beg sc.

Rnd 12: In next ch-3 sp work (sl st, ch 1, sc); * † ch 3, sc in next ch-3 sp, ch 3, 3 dc in next ch-3 sp; ch 7, (sc in next ch-7 sp, ch 7) twice; 3 sc in next ch-5 sp (near the ch-12 sp); in next ch-12 sp work (3 sc, ch 3, 3 sc, ch 5, 3 sc, ch 3, 3 sc); 3 sc in next ch-5 sp (near the ch-12 sp), ch 7; (sc in next ch-7 sp, ch 7) twice; 3 dc in next ch-3 sp †; ch 3, sc in next ch-3 sp; rep from * two times more, then rep from † to † one more time; ch 1, hdc in beg sc.

Rnd 13: Ch 1, sc in sp formed by joining hdc, ch 7, skip next ch-3 sp, sc in next ch-3 sp, ch 7; * † (sc in next ch-7 sp, ch 7) 3 times; sc in next ch-3 sp, ch 7, sc in next ch-5 sp, ch 7, sc in next ch-3 sp, ch 7; (sc in next ch-7 sp, ch 7) 3 times †; sc in next ch-3 sp, ch 7, skip next ch-3 sp, sc in next ch-3 sp, ch 7; rep from * two times more, then rep from † to † once; sl st in beg sc. Finish off; weave in ends.

SECOND SQUARE

Rep Rnds 1 through 12 of First Square. On next rnd, Second Square will be joined to First Square.

Rnd 13: Ch 1, sc in sp formed by joining hdc, ch 7, skip next ch-3 sp, sc in next ch-3 sp, ch 7, (sc in next ch-7 sp, ch 7) 3 times; sc in next ch-3 sp, ch 7, se in next ch-5 sp, ch 3; hold wrong sides of completed square and this square tog, and carefully matching sts, join as follows: on completed square, sl st in corresponding ch-7 sp, ch 3; on working square, sc in next ch-3 sp; † ch 3, on completed square, sl st in next ch-7 sp, ch 3; on working square, sc in next ch-7 sp †; rep from † to † twice more; ch 3; on completed square, sl st in next ch-7 sp, ch 3; on working square, sc in next ch-3 sp, ch 3; on completed square, sl st in next ch-7 sp, ch 3; on working square, skip next ch-3 sp, sc in next ch-3 sp; rep from † to † 3 times more, ch 3; on completed square, sl st in next ch-7 sp, ch 3; on working square, sc in next ch-3 sp, ch 3; on completed square, sl st in next ch-7 sp, ch 3; on working square, sc in next ch-5 sp; †† ch 7, sc in next ch-3 sp, ch 7, (sc in next ch-7 sp, ch 7) 3 times; sc in next ch-3 sp, ch 7, skip next ch-3 sp, se in next ch-3 sp, ch 7; (sc in next ch-7 sp, ch 7) 3 times; sc in next ch-3 sp, ch 7, sc in next ch-5 sp

††; rep from †† to †† once more; ch 7, sc in next ch-3 sp, ch 7, (sc in next ch-7 sp, ch 7) 3 times; sl st in beg sc. Finish off; weave in ends.

THIRD SQUARE (TWO-SIDED JOINING)

Work same as First Square through Rnd 12. On following rnd, Third Square will be joined on 2 sides.

Rnd 13: Ch 1, sc in sp formed by joining hdc, ch 7, skip next ch-3 sp, sc in next ch-3 sp, ch 7; (sc in next ch-7 sp, ch 7) 3 times; sc in next ch-3 sp, ch 7, se in next ch-5 sp; * ch 3; hold completed square and working square with wrong sides tog, and carefully matching sts, join as follows: on completed square, sl st in corresponding ch-7 sp, ch 3; on working square, sc in next ch-3 sp, † ch 3; on completed square, sl st in next ch-7 sp, ch 3; on working square, sc in next ch-7 sp †; rep from † to † twice more; ch 3, on completed square sl st in next ch-7 sp, ch 3; on working square, sc in next ch-3 sp, ch 3; on completed square, sl st in next ch-7 sp, ch 3; on working square, skip next ch-3 sp, sc in next ch-3 sp; rep from † to † 3 times; ch 3; on completed square, sl st in next ch-7 sp, ch 3; on working square, sc in next ch-3 sp, ch 3; on completed square, sl st in next ch-7 lp, ch 3; on working square, sc in next ch-5 lp; rep from * once more; ch 7, sc in next ch-3 sp, ch 7, (sc in next ch-7 lp, ch 7) 3 times; sc in next ch-3 sp, ch 7, skip next ch-3 sp, sc in next ch-3 sp, ch 7, (sc in next ch-7 lp, ch 7) 3 times; se in next ch-3 sp, ch 7, sc in next ch-5 lp, ch 7, sc in next ch-3 sp, ch 7, (sc in next ch-7 lp, ch 7) 3 times; sl st in beg sc. Finish off; weave in ends.

Additional Squares

Work as many squares as needed, joining all squares in the same manner as Second and Third squares, joining sides in the same way and working corner joins as needed. Be sure to join with the correct number of squares in the width and in the length of the piece.

When all squares are joined, work border.

BORDER

BORDER

With right side facing and one short end at top, join thread with sc in ch-7 lp in upper right-hand corner.

Rnd 1: Ch 4, sc in next sp, ch 4; in next sp work (CL, ch 5) 3 times; * (sc in next sp, ch 5) two times; in next sp work (CL, ch 5) 3 times; rep from * around, ending last rep as needed; sl st in beg sc. Finish off.

Rnd 2: Join with sc in any ch-5 lp; ch 5, * sc in next ch-5 lp, ch 5; rep from * around; sl st in beg sc. Finish off; weave in ends. Block if needed.

Butterfly Filet Table Topper

Pretty butterflies surround a dramatic center motif in this little table topper.

SIZE: 31½" diameter between sides; 33" diameter between points

MATERIALS

Size 10 crochet cotton,
  4 balls (400 yds each) or 1,600 yds natural
Size 7 (1.65 mm) steel crochet hook
  (or size required for gauge)

GAUGE

Rnds 1 through 4 = 2⅜" diameter between sides;
  2½" between points
Rnds 1 through 7 = 3¾" diameter between sides;
  4¼" between points

SPECIAL STITCHES

V-stitch (V-st): Work (dc, ch 3, dc) in specified st: V-st made.

Instructions

Starting in center, ch 4, join with sl st to form a ring.

Rnd 1 (right side): Ch 5 (counts as dc and ch-2 sp now and throughout); *dc in ring, ch 2; rep from * 6 times more: 8 dc and 8 ch-2 sps; join with sl st in 3rd ch of beg ch-5.

Rnd 2: Ch 6 (counts as dc and ch-3 sp of first V-st), dc in same ch as joining (first V-st made), ch 2; *V-st in next dc, ch 2; rep from * around: 8 V-sts and 8 ch-2 sps; join with sl st in 3rd ch of beg ch-6.

Rnd 3: Sl st in next ch and in ch-3 sp, ch 5; *(dc in next dc, ch 2) 2 times**; dc in next ch-3 sp, ch 2; rep from * around, ending final rep at **: 24 dc and 24 ch-2 sps; join with sl st in 3rd ch of beg ch-5.

Rnd 4: Ch 4 (counts as dc and ch-1 sp now and throughout), dc in same ch as joining, ch 2; *(dc in next dc, ch 2) 2 times**; (dc, ch 1, dc) in next dc, ch 2; rep from * around, ending final rep at **: 32 dc, 24 ch-2 sps and 8 ch-1 sps; join with sl st in 3rd ch of beg ch-4.

Rnd 5: Ch 6 (counts as dc and ch-3 sp); *dc in next dc, ch 2; dc in next dc, 2 dc in next ch-2 sp, dc in next dc, ch 2**; dc in next dc, ch 3; rep from * around, ending final rep at **: 48 dc, 8 ch-3 sps and 16 ch-2 sps; join with sl st in 3rd ch of beg ch-6.

110

Rnd 6: Sl st in next ch and in ch-3 sp, ch 5; *dc in next dc, ch 2, dc in next 4 dc, ch 2, dc in next dc, ch 2**; dc in next ch-3 sp, ch 2; rep from * around, ending final rep at **: 56 dc and 32 ch-2 sps; join with sl st in 3rd ch of beg ch-5.

Rnd 7: Ch 6 (counts as dc and ch-3 sp of first V-st), dc in same ch as joining (first V-st made), ch 2; *dc in next dc, 2 dc in next ch-2 sp, dc in next dc, ch 2**; skip next 2 dc, rep from * to ** once***; V-st in next dc, ch 2; rep from * around, ending final rep at ***: 8 V-sts, 64 dc and 24 ch-2 sps; join with sl st in 3rd ch of beg ch-6.

Rnd 8: Sl st in next ch and in ch-3 sp, ch 5; *dc in next dc, ch 2, (dc in next 4 dc, ch 2) 2 times; dc in next dc, ch 2**; dc in next ch-3 sp, ch 2; rep from * around, ending final rep at **: 88 dc and 40 ch-2 sps; join with sl st in 3rd ch of beg ch-5.

Rnd 9: Ch 4, dc in same ch as joining, ch 2; *dc in next dc, 2 dc in next ch-2 sp, dc in next dc, ch 2**; (dc, ch 5, dc) in next ch-2 sp, ch 2**; skip next 3 dc, rep from * to ** once***; (dc, ch 1, dc) in next dc, ch 2; rep from * around, ending final rep at ***: 96 dc, 8 ch-5 lps, 32 ch-2 sps and 8 ch-1 sps; join with sl st in 3rd ch of beg ch-4.

Rnd 10: Ch 6 (counts as dc and ch-3 sp); *dc in next dc, ch 2, dc in next 4 dc, ch 4, 2 sc in next ch-5 lp, ch 4, skip next dc, dc in next 4 dc, ch 2**; dc in next dc, ch 3; rep from * around, ending final rep at **: 80 dc, 16 sc, 16 ch-4 lps, 8 ch-3 sps and 16 ch-2 sps; join with sl st in 3rd ch of beg ch-6.

Rnd 11: Sl st in next ch and in ch-3 sp, ch 5; *dc in next dc, 2 dc in next ch-2 sp, dc in next dc**; ch 5, sc in next ch-4 lp, sc in next 2 sc, sc in next ch-4 lp, ch 5; skip next 3 dc; rep from * to ** once***, ch 2***; dc in next ch-3 sp, ch 2; rep from * around, ending final rep at ***: 72 dc, 32 sc, 16 ch-5 lps and 16 ch-2 sps; join with sl st in 3rd ch of beg ch-5.

Rnd 12: Ch 4, dc in same ch as joining, ch 2; *dc in next 4 dc; ch 4, 2 sc in next ch-5 lp, sc in next 4 sc, 2 sc in next ch-5 lp, ch 4; dc in next 4 dc, ch 2**; (dc, ch 1, dc) in next dc, ch 2; rep from * around, ending final rep at **: 80 dc, 64 sc, 16 ch-4 lps, 16 ch-2 sps and 8 ch-1 sps; join with sl st in 3rd ch of beg ch-4.

Rnd 13: Ch 6 (counts as dc and ch-3 sp); *dc in next dc, 2 dc in next ch-2 sp, dc in next dc**; ch 6, 2 sc in next ch-4 lp, sc in next 8 sc, 2 sc in next ch-4 lp, ch 6; skip next 3 dc***; rep from * to ** once; ch 3; rep from * around, ending final rep at ***; dc in next dc, 2 dc in next ch-2 sp: 64 dc, 96 sc, 16 ch-6 lps and 8 ch-3 sps; join with sl st in 3rd ch of beg ch-6.

Rnd 14: Sl st in next ch and in ch-3 sp, ch 5; *dc in next 4 dc, ch 7, sc in next ch-6 lp, sc in next 2 sc, ch 6, skip next 8 sc, sc in next 2 sc, sc in next ch-6 lp, ch 7; dc in next 4 dc, ch 2**; dc in next ch-3 sp, ch 2; rep from * around, ending final rep at **: 72 dc, 48 sc, 16 ch-7 lps, 8 ch-6 lps and 16 ch-2 sps; join with sl st in 3rd ch of beg ch-5.

Rnd 15: Ch 6 (counts as dc and ch-3 sp of first V-st), dc in same ch as joining (first V-st made), ch 2; *dc in next dc, ch 2; skip next 2 dc, dc in next dc**; 3 dc in next ch-7 lp; ch 7, skip next 2 sc, sc in next sc, 6 sc in next ch-6 lp, sc in next sc, ch 7; 3 dc in next ch-7 lp; rep from * to ** once; ch 2***; V-st in next dc, ch 2; rep from * around, ending final rep at ***: 8 V-sts, 80 dc, 64 sc, 16 ch-7 lps and 32 ch-2 sps; join with sl st in 3rd ch of beg ch-6.

Rnd 16: Sl st in next ch and in ch-3 sp, ch 5; *(dc in next dc, ch 2) 3 times; skip next 2 dc, dc in next dc, 3 dc in next ch-7 lp, ch 8, skip next 3 sc, sc in next 2 sc, ch 8, 3 dc in next ch-7 lp, dc in next dc, ch 2, skip next 2 dc**; (dc in next dc, ch 2) 3 times**; dc in next ch-3 sp, ch 2; rep from * around, ending final rep at **: 120 dc, 16 sc, 16 ch-8 lps and 64 ch-2 sps: join with sl st in 3rd ch of beg ch-5.

Rnd 17: Ch 4, dc in same ch as joining, ch 2; *dc in next dc, 2 dc in next ch-2 sp, dc in next dc, ch 2**; (dc in next dc, ch 2) 2 times; skip next 2 dc, dc in next dc, 3 dc in next ch-8 lp, ch 2, 3 dc in next ch-8 lp, dc in next dc, ch 2, skip next 2 dc, (dc in next dc, ch 2) 2 times; rep from * to ** once***; (dc, ch 1, dc) in next dc, ch 2; rep from * around, ending final rep at ***: 176 dc, 72 ch-2 sps and 8 ch-1 sps; join with sl st in 3rd ch of beg ch-4.

Rnds 18 through 62: Work open mesh, closed mesh and lacets as per chart and filet instructions on pages 134-138. Work beg, corners and end of rnds as follows:

Rnds 18, 21, 26, 29, 34, 37, 42, 45, 50 and 53: Work [ch 6 (counts as dc and ch-3 sp), dc in next dc] at beg, [ch 3, dc in next dc] in corners and [omit final dc of last mesh, join with sl st in 3rd ch of beg ch-6] at end.

Rnds 19, 22, 24, 27, 30, 32, 35, 38, 40, 43, 46, 48, 51, 54 and 56: Work [sl st in next ch and in ch-3 sp, ch 5 (counts as dc and ch-2 sp), dc in next dc] at beg, [ch 2, dc in next ch-3 sp, ch 2, dc in next dc] in corners and [ch 2, join with sl st in 3rd ch of beg ch-5] at end.

Rnds 20, 25, 28, 33, 36, 41, 44, 49 and 52: Work [ch 4 (counts as dc and ch-1 sp), dc in same ch as joining] at beg, [ch 1, dc in same dc as last dc] in corners and [omit final dc of last mesh, join with sl st in 3rd ch of beg ch-4] at end.

Rnds 23, 31, 39, 47 and 55: Work [ch 6 (counts as dc and ch-3 sp), dc in same ch as joining] at beg, [ch 3, dc in same dc as last dc] in corners and [omit final dc of last mesh, join with sl st in 3rd ch of beg ch-6] at end.

Rnd 57: Work [ch 3, dc in same ch as joining] at beg, [dc in same dc as last dc] in corners and [omit final dc of last mesh, join with sl st in 3rd ch of beg ch-3] at end.

Rnd 58: Work [ch 3, dc in next dc] at beg, [dc in next dc] in corners and [omit final dc of last mesh, join with sl st in 3rd ch of beg ch-3] at end.

Rnd 59: Work [ch 5 (counts as dc and ch-2 sp), dc in next dc] at beg, [ch 2, dc in next dc] in corners and [omit final dc of last mesh, join with sl st in 3rd ch of beg ch-5] at end.

Rnd 60: Work [sl st in next ch-2 sp, ch 6 (counts as dc and ch-3 sp), dc in same ch-2 sp, dc in next dc] at beg, [(dc, ch 3, dc) in next ch-2 sp, dc in next dc] in corners and [join with sl st in 3rd ch of beg ch-6] at end.

Rnd 61: Work [sl st in next ch-3 sp, ch 3, 3 dc in same ch-3 sp, dc in next 2 dc] at beg, [dc in next dc, 4 dc in next ch-3 sp, dc in next 2 dc] in corners and [dc in next dc, join with sl st in 3rd ch of beg ch-3] at end.

Rnd 62: Work [sl st in next dc, ch 6 (counts as dc and ch-3 sp), dc in next dc, ch 2, skip next 2 dc, dc in next dc] at beg, [ch 2, skip next 2 dc, dc in next dc, ch 3, dc in next dc, ch 2, skip next 2 dc, dc in next dc] in corners and [ch 2, join with sl st in 3rd ch of beg ch-6] at end.

Rnd 63: Ch 1, sc in same ch as joining, ch 2, sc in next ch-3 sp, ch 2, sc in next dc; *ch 2, skip next 2 chs, sc in next dc; rep from * around, working [ch 2, sc in next ch-3 sp, ch 2, sc in next dc] in each corner ch-3 sp. Join with sl st in first sc. Finish off; weave in ends.

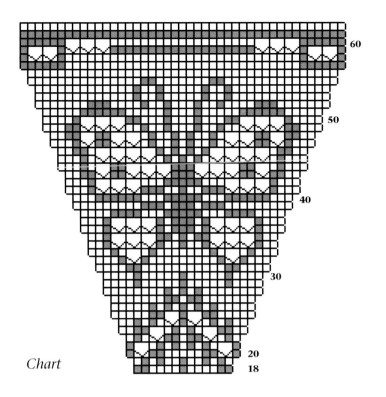

Chart

60

50

40

30

20
18

KEY

☐ open mesh

■ closed mesh

◇ lacets

Elegance for the Table

Blocks of stylized blossoms combine to make a truly elegant accent for your table.

SIZE: 60" x 68"

MATERIALS

Size 20 crochet thread

22 balls (400 yds each) or 8,800 yds ecru

Tapestry needle

Stitch markers

Size 11 (1.1 mm) steel crochet hook
   (or size required for gauge)

GAUGE

8-rnd motif = 4" x 4"

Rnds 1 through 5 = 2$\frac{1}{2}$" x 2$\frac{1}{2}$"

SPECIAL STITCHES

2 triple cluster (2 tr CL): *YO twice, insert hook in specified st or sp and draw up a lp, (YO and draw through 2 lps on hook) twice; rep from * once; YO and draw through all 3 lps on hook: 2 tr CL made.

Beginning 5 triple cluster (beg 5 tr CL): Ch 4, *YO twice, insert hook in specified st or sp and draw up a lp, (YO and draw through 2 lps on hook) twice; rep from * 3 times more; YO and draw through all 5 lps on hook: beg 5 tr CL made.

5 triple cluster (5 tr CL): *YO twice, insert hook in specified st or sp and draw up a lp, (YO and draw through 2 lps on hook) twice; rep from * 4 times more; YO and draw through all 6 lps on hook: 5 tr CL made.

Motif

Instructions

MOTIF (MAKE 255)

Ch 8; join with sl st to form a ring.

Rnd 1 (right side): Ch 4 (counts as tr), 23 tr in ring: 24 tr; join with sl st in 4th ch of beg ch-4.

Rnd 2: Ch 6 (counts as a dc and ch-3 sp); *skip next tr, dc in back lp and back bar of next tr, ch 3; rep from * 10 times more: 12 dc and 12 ch-3 sps; join with sl st in 3rd ch of beg ch-6.

Rnd 3: Sl st in next ch-3 sp, ch 4 (counts as a tr), 4 tr in same ch-3 sp, ch 2; *5 tr in next ch-3 sp, ch 2; rep from * 10 times more: 60 tr and 12 ch-2 sps; join with sl st in 4th ch of beg ch-4.

116

Rnd 4: Ch 4, tr in back lp and back bar of next 4 tr, ch 3; *tr in back lp and back bar of next 5 tr, ch 3; rep from * 10 times more: 60 tr and 12 ch-3 sps; join as before.

Rnd 5: Work 5 tr CL in back lp and back bar of next 4 tr, ch 10; *5 tr CL in back lp and back bar of next 5 tr, ch 10; rep from * 10 times more: twelve 5 tr CL and 12 ch-10 sps; join with sl st in first tr CL.

Rnd 6: Ch 1, sc in same st as joining, ch 5; *(dc, ch 5) 4 times in next ch-10 sp, sc in next tr CL, ch 5; rep from * 10 times more; (dc, ch 5) 4 times in next ch-10 sp: 60 ch-5 sps, 48 dc and 12 sc; join with sl st in first sc.

Rnd 7: Sl st in 2nd ch of next ch-5 sp; *ch 5, (sc in next ch-5 sp, ch 5) 3 times, sl st in 4th ch of next ch-5 sp and in 2nd ch of following ch-5 sp tog; rep from * 11 times more omitting sl st at end of last rep: 48 ch-5 sps, 36 sc and 12 sl sts; join with sl st in 4th ch of next ch-5 sp and in first sl st tog.

Rnd 8: Sl st in next 2 chs, ch 4, tr in same ch-5 sp (beg 2 tr CL made), place marker in tr; *(ch 5, sc in next ch-5 sp) 2 times, ch 5, (2 tr CL in next ch-5 sp) 2 times, ch 5, turn; skip next ch-5 sp, 7 tr in next ch-5 sp, ch 5, sc in last marked st, ch 5, turn; tr in first 3 tr, (tr, ch 5, tr) in next tr, tr in next 3 tr, ch 5, sc in last tr CL; **(ch 5, sc in next ch-5 sp) 2 times, ch 5, (2 tr CL in next ch-5 sp) 2 times; rep from **once more; place marker in last tr dec; rep from * 3 times more omitting last tr CL: twenty-four 2 tr CL, 60 tr, 56 ch-5 sps and 32 sc; join with sl st in first tr CL. Finish off; weave in ends.

JOINING

Hold 2 motifs with right sides tog. With tapestry needle and thread, with overcast st sew motifs tog through back lps and back bars in 10 sts at each corner (from center ch of corner ch-5 sp to center ch of next ch-5 sp) and in center 20 sts on each side. Join into 15 rows of 17 motifs each.

EDGING

With right side facing, join thread with sl st in back lp and back bar of any st around edge, ch 3, dc in back lp and back bar of next st and in back lp and back bar of each st around edges, working 3 dc in back lp and back bar of center ch of corner ch-5 sp at 4 corners of tablecloth; join with sl st in 3rd ch of beg ch-3. Finish off; weave in ends.

Animals on Parade
Child's Spread

This clever spread was probably designed by Anne Orr, or someone in her employ (see page 28). Barnyard animals as well as cats, a dog—even an ostrich—play happily together on this heirloom-quality gift for a favorite child. The spread even includes numbers and an alphabet to help the little one learn. For a wall hanging, just leave off the borders.

SIZE: 28" x 53¹/₂" plus 4" wide edging on bottom and sides

MATERIALS

Size 20 crochet cotton,
    19 balls (400 yds each) or 7,600 yds white
Sizes 9 (1.40 mm) and
    11 (1.10 mm) steel crochet hooks
        (or sizes required for gauge)

GAUGE

With smaller hook; 21 mesh = 4";
    24 mesh rows = 4"
With larger hook; 20 mesh = 4";
    21 mesh rows = 4"

Instructions

ANIMAL BLOCKS
(make 15; one each of Charts 1 through 15)

With smaller hook, ch 126.

Row 1 (right side): Dc in 9th ch from hook; *ch 2, skip 2 chs, dc in next ch; rep from * across: 40 open mesh; ch 5, turn.

Rows 2 through 54: Work open and closed mesh as per Charts 1 through 15 and filet instructions on pages 134-138. At end of Row 54, finish off; weave in ends.

INSERTS
(make 10)

With smaller hook, ch 48.

Row 1(right side): Dc in 9th ch from hook; *ch 2, skip 2 chs, dc in next ch; rep from * across: 14 open mesh; ch 5, turn.

Rows 2 through 54: Work open and closed mesh as per Insert Chart and filet instructions on pages 134-138. At end of Row 54, finish off; weave in ends.

TOP SECTION

Note: *Use number and letter charts to graph out initials and dates as desired to personalize child spread. Suggestion: Model uses numbers and letters such as "APR 28 SLC 1949", which would signify someone with the initials of SLC being born on April 28, 1949. Insert graphed numbers and letters into chart of Top Section above and below charted zigzag, allowing for 3 rows of open mesh above top row of numbers and letters and 1 row of open mesh above bottom row of numbers and letters and below top and bottom rows of numbers and letters.*

With smaller hook, ch 450.

Row 1 (right side): Dc in 9th ch from hook; *ch 2, skip 2 chs, dc in next ch; rep from * across: 148 open mesh; ch 5, turn.

Rows 2 through 51: Work open and closed mesh as per Top Section Chart with numbers and letters added and filet instructions on pages 134-138. At end of Row 51, finish off; weave in ends.

BOTTOM EDGING

With larger hook, ch 52.

Row 1 (right side): Dc in 5th ch from hook, dc in next 2 chs; *ch 2, skip 2 chs, dc in next 4 chs; rep from * 6 times more; ch 2, skip 2 chs, dc in last ch: 8 open mesh and 8 closed mesh; ch 5, turn.

Rows 2 through 149: Work open and closed mesh as per Bottom Edging Chart and filet instructions on pages 134-138. At end of Row 149, finish off; weave in ends.

SIDE EDGINGS

(make 2)

Starting at bottom with smaller hook, ch 54.

Row 1 (right side on right side edge and wrong side on left side edge): Dc in 9th ch from hook; *dc in next 3 chs, ch 2, skip 2 chs, dc in next ch; rep from * across to last 3 chs; ch 2, skip 2 chs, dc in last ch: 9 open mesh and 7 closed mesh; ch 5, turn.

Rows 2 through 102: Work open and closed mesh as per Side Edgings Chart and filet instructions on pages 134-138.

Rep Rows 3 through 102 two times more, then work Rows 103 through 121. At end of last row, finish off; weave in ends.

ASSEMBLY

With right sides of Animal Blocks, Inserts and Top Section facing, arrange according to Assembly Diagram on page 131 or as desired with Top Section at top and 3 columns of 5 Animal Blocks with 2 columns of 5 Inserts between them at bottom. Whip stitch edges of pieces together. Whip stitch straight side and bottom edges of assembled center section and edgings together with right sides facing (except for wrong side of Left Side Edging).

Note: *Ease in one extra row of Bottom Edging along bottom edge of center section.*

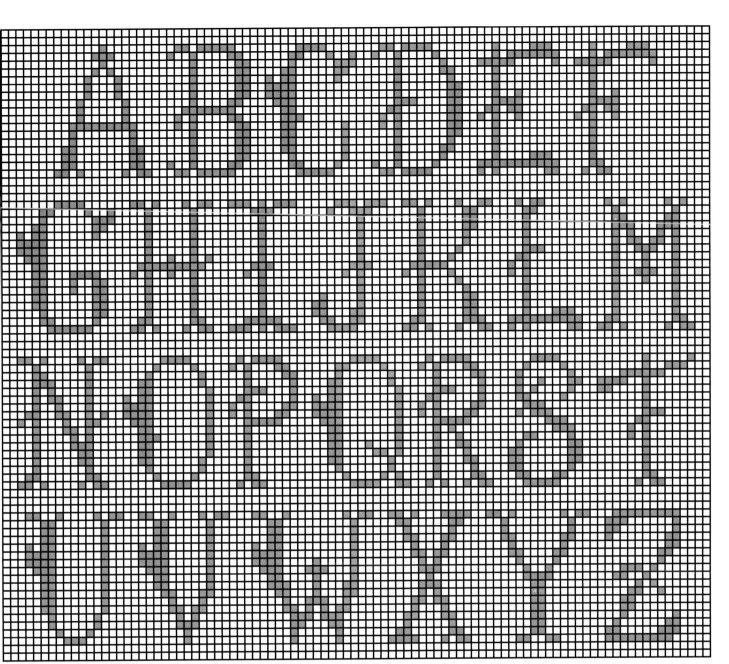

Letters

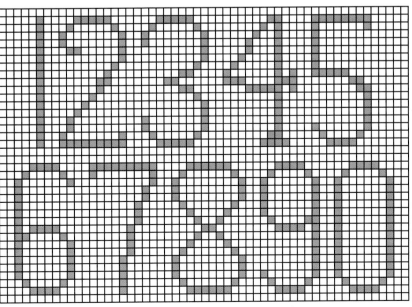

Numbers

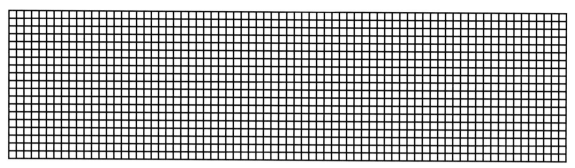

Graph Paper Left

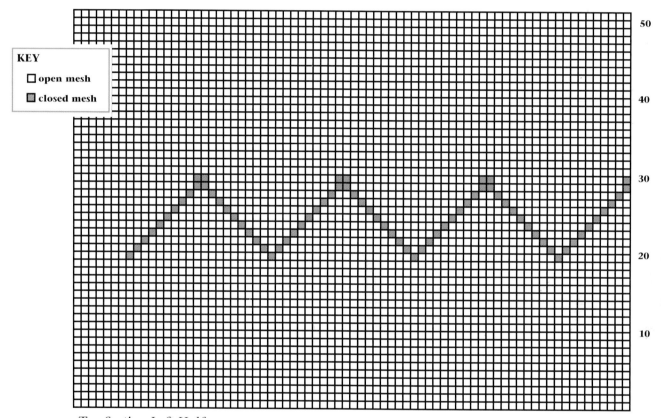

KEY
☐ open mesh
▨ closed mesh

50

40

30

20

10

Top Section Left Half

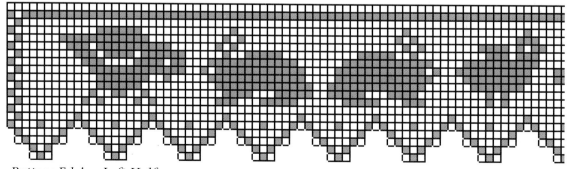

Bottom Edging Left Half

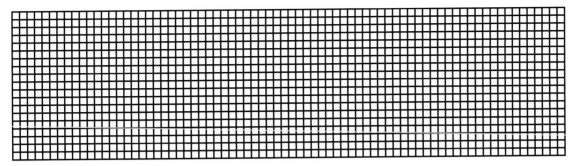

Graph Paper Right

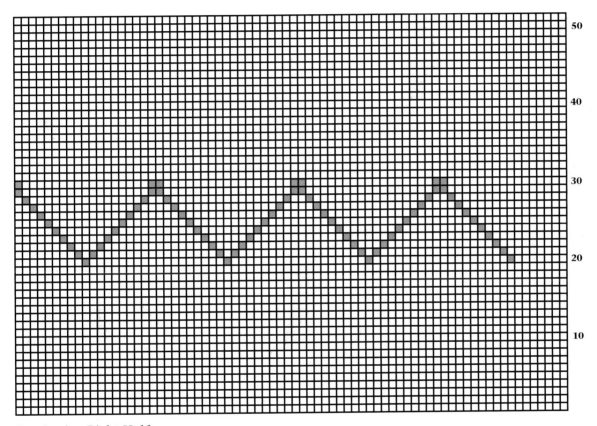

50

40

30

20

10

Top Section Right Half

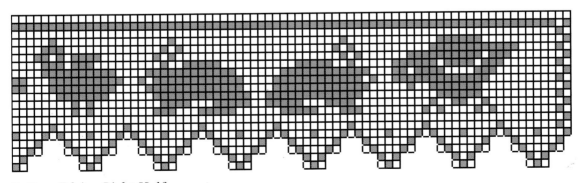

Bottom Edging Right Half

125

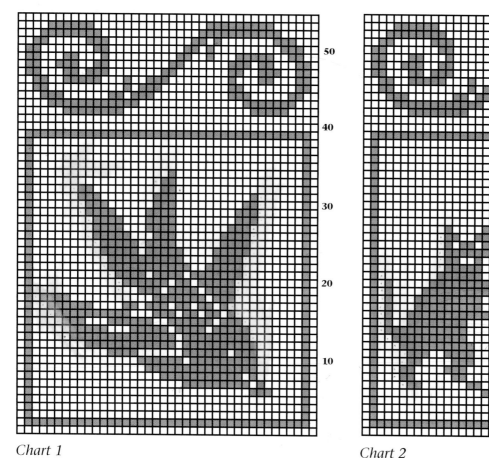

Chart 1

Chart 2

KEY

☐ open mesh
▨ closed mesh

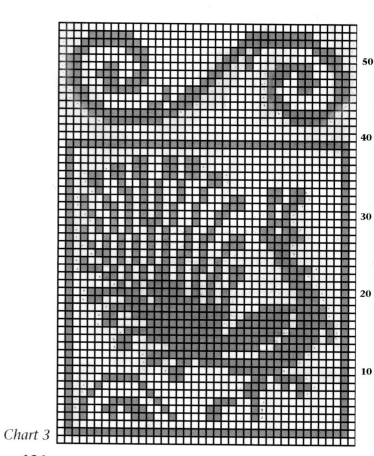

Chart 3

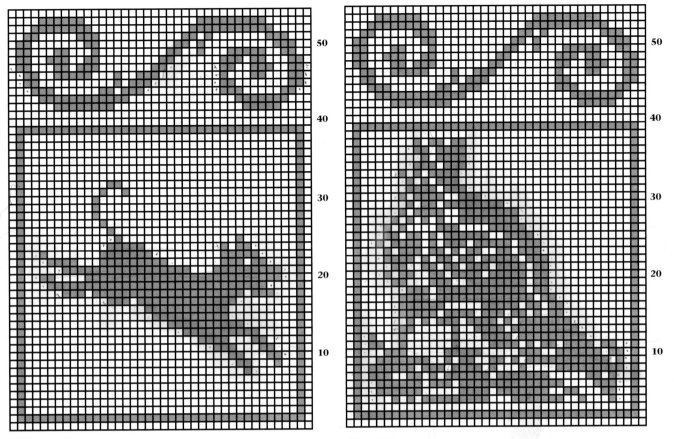

Chart 4

Chart 5

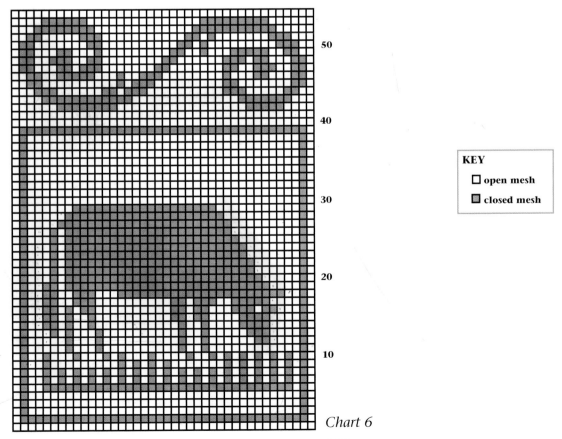

KEY

□ open mesh

■ closed mesh

Chart 6

127

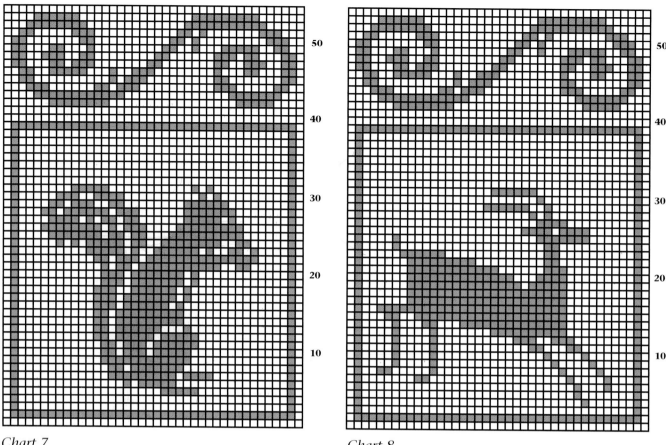

Chart 7

Chart 8

KEY

□ open mesh

▨ closed mesh

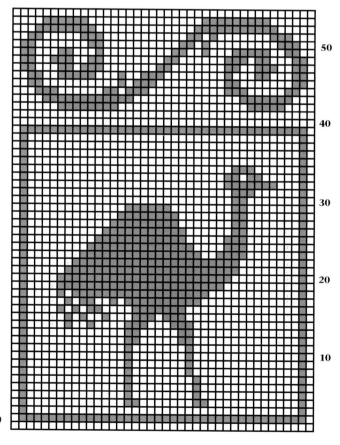

Chart 9

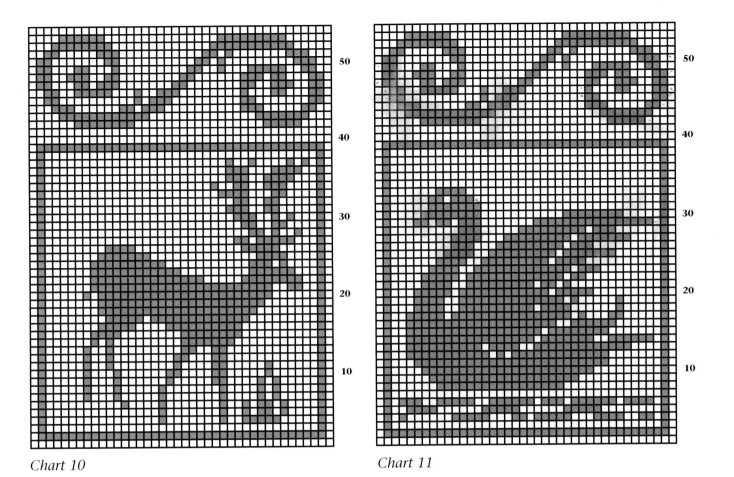

Chart 10

Chart 11

50

40

30

20

10

50

40

30

20

10

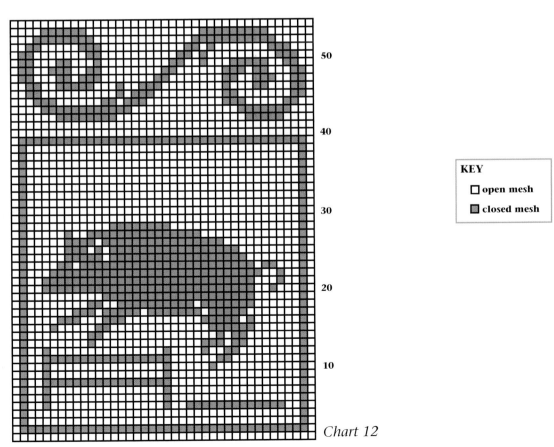

50

40

30

20

10

KEY

☐ open mesh

☐ closed mesh

Chart 12

129

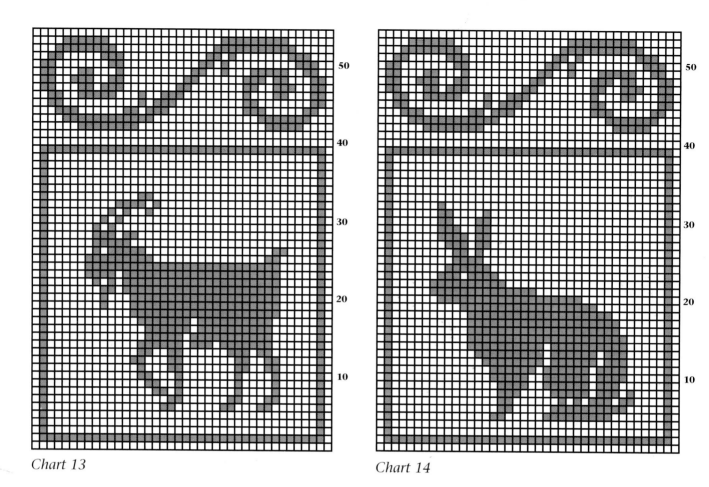

Chart 13

Chart 14

KEY

☐ open mesh

■ closed mesh

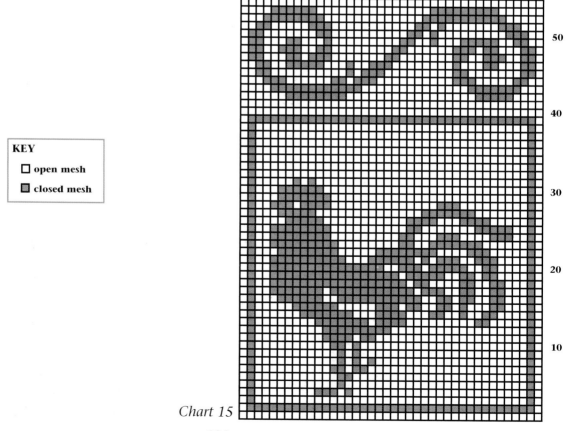

Chart 15

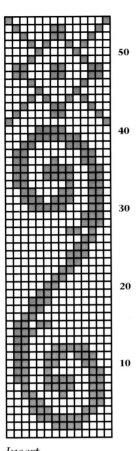

Insert

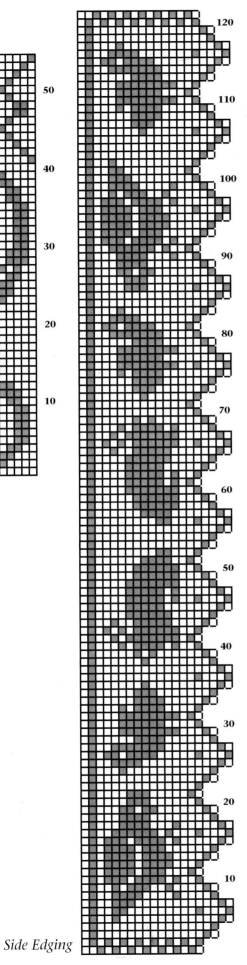

Side Edging

Top Section				
Chart 15	Insert	Chart 10	Insert	Chart 5
Chart 14	Insert	Chart 9	Insert	Chart 4
Chart 13	Insert	Chart 8	Insert	Chart 3
Chart 12	Insert	Chart 7	Insert	Chart 2
Chart 11	Insert	Chart 6	Insert	Chart 1

Assembly Diagram

131

GENERAL DIRECTIONS

Crocheting with a Steel Hook

Even an experienced crocheter may feel clumsy and awkward at first when working with steel hooks for the first time. This might be a bit of a surprise especially if you have been crocheting with yarn for a long time; you may feel all thumbs all over again just as you felt when you first learned to crochet. However, in just a few hours of crocheting with a steel hook and thread, this feeling will pass as you learn to adjust your tension and method of working to these new tools.

Most steel crochet hooks are about 5" long, which is shorter than the hooks you use for yarn. Steel hooks are numbered from 14, which is the smallest, to 00, which is the largest. You will find that the steel hook is shaped differently than the hooks you have been using.

After the end, used to hook the thread, there is the throat, then the shank, and after the shank the steel hook begins to widen again before it reaches the finger grip. It is important that every stitch be made on the shank, not the throat. That would make the stitch too tight. If your stitches slide beyond the shank, they will be loose and alter the gauge.

Hold the hook in the right hand (unless you are left-handed), with the thumb and the third finger on the fingertip and the index finger near the tip of the hook. Turn the hook slightly toward you, not facing up or down. Hold the hook firmly, but not tightly.

Steel crochet hooks are numbered differently in the United States, and the rest of the world. Below is a chart which will help to establish the difference.

throat   shank

Steel Crochet Hooks Conversion Chart

U.S.	00	0	1	2	3	4	5	6	7	8	9	10	11	12	13	14
Metric	3.5	3.25	2.75	2.25	2.1	2	1.9	1.8	1.65	1.5	1.4	1.3	1.1	1.0	0.85	0.75

Crochet Thread

The thread used for crochet comes in a number of sizes from very fine crochet cotton used for making lace or tatting to sizes 20 and 10, used most often for doilies and bedspreads. The larger the number, the finer the thread. Size 10, called bedspread weight, is the thread most commonly used (and the one that is used for most of the projects in this book).

Crochet thread is produced by various manufacturers and sold under a number of brand names. The labels on the thread will tell you how much thread in ounces, grams, meters and yards is in the ball. It will also tell you about the fiber content of the thread—usually cotton—and its washability. The label will also give you the dye lot number of the particular ball or skein. The same color—even white or ecru—can vary from dye lot to dye lot. Make certain that all of the thread used for a project is from the same dye lot. Otherwise you may notice variations in color when the project is completed.

Finishing a Project

You may wish to wash a project when it is completed. If so, do so by hand, using a mild soap. Rinse it well in warm water, then block it while still damp.

Blocking will set the project into its final size or shape. Spread the project out on a flat surface, with the right side up. For the large projects, you may need to block on a sheet placed on the floor or on a bed. If the project is not already damp from laundering, you will need to spray it with water. Pat the project out to the size you want, being sure to square off the design. Then pin in place with rust-proof pins. You may wish to spray lightly with a spray starch to help retain the shape. Leave the project pinned in place until it is completely dry, which in sultry weather may take several days.

Thread projects have a more finished look when they are starched with a stiffening solution. Commercial stiffening solutions are available at your local craft or needlework department or store. You can also make a stiffening solution from equal amounts of white craft glue and water.

Pour the stiffening solution into a plastic bag, and place the bag in a bowl. After you have washed and rinsed your thread project, immerse it into the solution. Allow the project to remain in the solution for about a minute. Then remove it, and press out the excess liquid. Don't squeeze. The project needs to be very wet, but no solution should be sitting in any of the holes.

Now spread the project out on the flat surface and pin it into shape, using only rust-proof pins. If you are planning to do many thread projects, you might want to invest in a blocking board. Making certain that the right side is up, smooth the project out to its proper size. Make sure that all of the loops and swirls are open and in their right positions. Allow your project to dry; removing the pins only when the project is completely dry. If you cover your board with some plastic wrap, the completed project will be easier to remove.

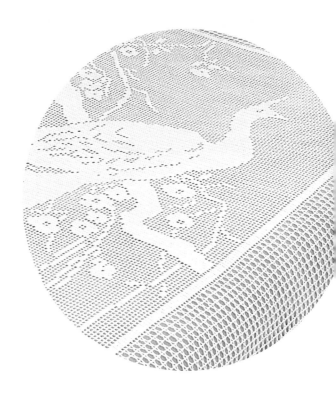

Working Filet Projects

Many of the projects in this book are worked in filet crochet, a technique that lets you create beautiful designs with easy basic stitches. Filet crochet is formed with squares, some open, and some closed, called closed mesh and open mesh (or sometimes blocks and spaces). It is worked by following charts, which are much easier to follow than written instructions.

Here is a close-up photo of an actual filet piece, which shows the structure of the design.

And here is the chart that was used to work the piece. You can see that the chart is almost the exact image of the actual worked piece.

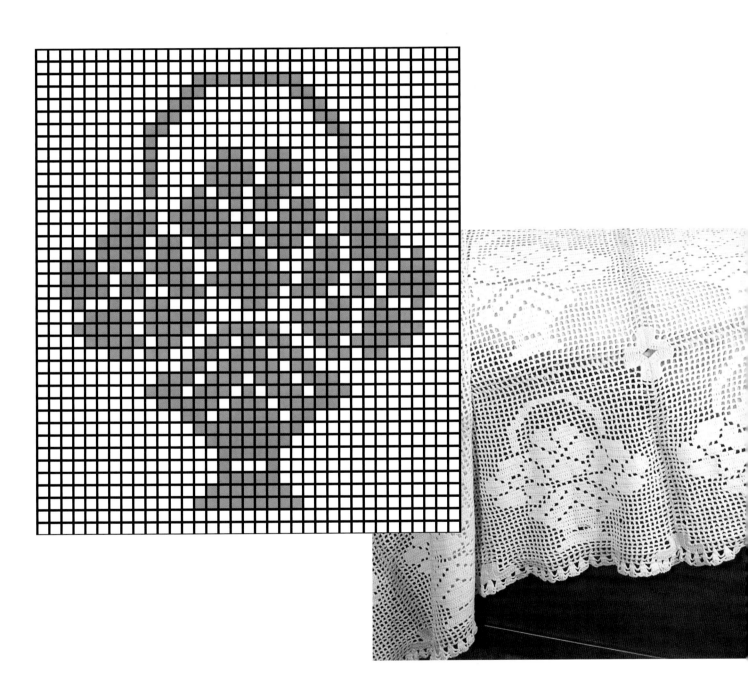

Reading the Charts

On our charts, a blank square stands for an **open mesh**, and a filled-in square stands for a closed mesh.

An open mesh is made with a dc, then 2 chs, then another dc.

The chart for open meshes will look like this.

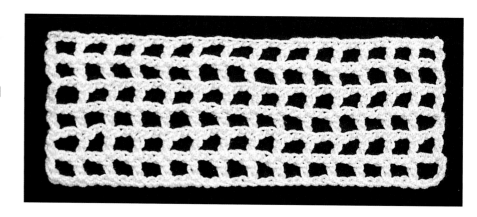

To start a row, form the first dc and ch-2 sp by working a ch 5 at the end of the preceding row. This ch 5 equals a dc and a ch-2 sp. To end the row, work the final dc into the third ch of the ch-5 turning ch.

A **closed mesh** is made by 4 dc sts: one on each side and 2 in the middle. To work a closed mesh over an open mesh on the previous row, work: dc in next dc, 2 dc in ch-2 sp, dc in next dc. To work a closed mesh over a closed mesh on the previous row, work: dc next 4 dc.

A chart showing closed meshes will look like this.

closed mesh   open mesh

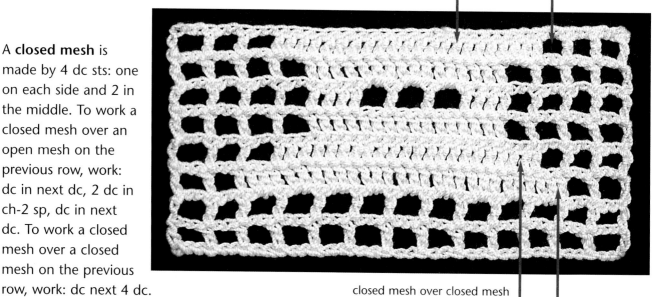

closed mesh over closed mesh

closed mesh
over an
open mesh

Increasing and Decreasing

In some designs, you will be increasing or decreasing the number of closed meshes or open meshes at the edges.

Increases are made by working additional chs, as specified in the pattern, in the turning ch at the end of a row to add blocks for the next row.

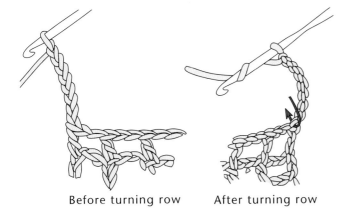

Before turning row   After turning row

To add open meshes at the end of the working row, work a ch 2, then a dtr (YO 3 times) in the same place as last dc was made .

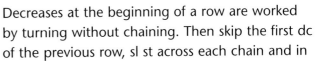
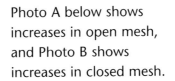

top

Photo A below shows increases in open mesh, and Photo B shows increases in closed mesh.

Decreases at the beginning of a row are worked by turning without chaining. Then skip the first dc of the previous row, sl st across each chain and in each dc until you reach the first block that will be worked. A decrease at the end of a row is made by working the last block shown on the chart, then turning, leaving the following blocks unworked.

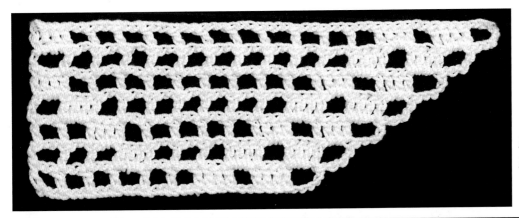

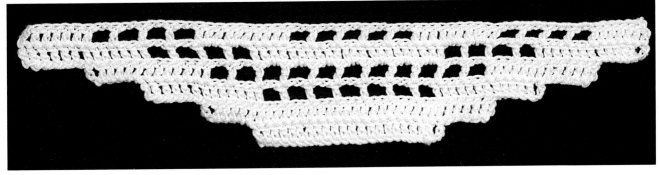

Photo A
Increases in open mesh

Photo B Increases in closed mesh

Lacets

A lacet is a decorative stitch that is shown on the charts by this symbol.

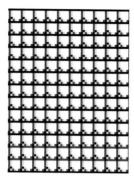

A lacet covers two open or closed meshes and two rows, and is worked like this: Dc in next dc, ch 3, skip next 2 sts, sc in next st, ch 3, skip next 2 sts, dc in next st (see photo). To work the next row above a lacet, dc in first dc of lacet, ch 5, dc in next dc as shown in photo.

Working from the Charts

The first row of each chart is read from right to left, the second row from left to right. Continue alternating directions with each row.

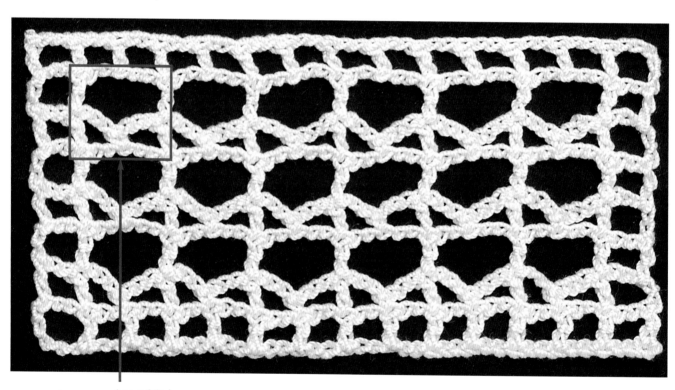

Lacet Stitch

Abbreviations and Symbols

Crochet patterns are written in a special shorthand which is used so that instructions don't take up too much space. They sometimes seem confusing, but once you learn them, you'll have no trouble following them.

BB	bobble
Beg	beginning
BP	back post
BP Edc	Back post extended double crochet
Cl(s)	cluster(s)
Ch(s)	chain(s)
Cont	continue
Dc	double crochet
Dc dec	double crochet decrease
Dec	decrease
Dtr	double triple crochet
Dtr cl	double triple crochet cluster
Dtr dec	double triple crochet decrease
Edc	extended double crochet
Edc cl	exended double crochet cluster
Fig	figure
FP	front post
FP Edc	front post extended double crochet
G	grams
Inc	Increase(ing)
Lp(s)	loop(s)
Patt	pattern
PC	popcorn
Prev	previous
Rem	remaining
Rep	repeat(ing)
Rnd(s)	round(s)
Sc	single crochet
Sc dec	single crochet decrease
Sl st	slip stitch
Sp(s)	space(s)

St(s)	stitch(es)
Tog	together
Tr	triple crochet
Tr dec	triple crochet decrease
Tr tr	triple triple crochet
V-st	V-stitch
YO	yarn over hook

THESE ARE STANDARD SYMBOLS

* An asterisk (or double asterisks**) in a pattern row, indicates a portion of instructions to be used more than once. For instance, "rep from * three times" means that after working the instructions once, you must work them again three times for a total of 4 times in all.

† A dagger (or double daggers ††) indicates that those instructions will be repeated again later in the same row or round.

: The number of stitches after a colon tells you the number of stitches you will have when you have completed the row or round.

( ) Parentheses enclose instructions which are to be worked the number of times following the parentheses. For instance, "(ch 1, sc, ch 1) 3 times" means that you will chain one, work one single crochet, and then chain again three times for a total of 6 chains and 3 single crochets.

Parentheses often set off or clarify a group of stitches to be worked into the same space or stitch. For instance, "(dc, ch 2, dc) in corner sp".

[ ] Brackets and ( ) parentheses are also used to give you additional information.

Terms

Front Loop–This is the loop toward you at the top of the crochet stitch.

Back Loop–This is the loop away from you at the top of the crochet stitch.

Post–This is the vertical part of the crochet stitch.

Join–This means to join with a sl st unless another stitch is specified.

Finish Off–This means to end your piece by pulling the cut yarn end through the last loop remaining on the hook. This will prevent the work from unraveling.

Continue in Pattern as Established–This means to follow the pattern stitch as it has been set up, working any increases or decreases in such a way that the pattern remains the same as it was established.

Work even–This means that the work is continued in the pattern as established without increasing or decreasing.

The patterns in this book have been written using the crochet terminology that is used in the United States. Terms which may have different equivalents in other parts of the world are listed below.

United States	International
Double crochet (dc)	treble crochet (tr)
Gauge	tension
Half double crochet (hdc)	half treble crochet (htr)
Single crochet	double crochet
Skip	miss
Slip stitch	single crochet
Triple crochet (tr)	double treble crochet (dtr)
Yarn over (YO)	yarn forward (yfwd)

Gauge

This is probably the most important aspect of crocheting!

GAUGE simply means the number of stitches per inch, and the numbers of rows per inch that result from a specified yarn worked with a hook in a specified size. But since everyone crochets differently—some loosely, some tightly, some in between—the measurements of individual work can vary greatly, even when the crocheters use the same pattern and the same size thread and hook.

If you don't work to the gauge specified in the pattern, your project will never be the correct size, and you may not have enough thread to finish your project. The hook size given in the instructions is merely a guide and should never be used without a gauge swatch.

To make a gauge swatch, crochet a swatch that is about 4" square, using the suggested hook and the number of stitches given in the pattern. Measure your swatch. If the number of stitches is fewer than those listed in the pattern, try making another swatch with a smaller hook. If the number of stitches is more than is called for in the pattern, try making another swatch with a larger hook. It is your responsibility to make sure you achieve the gauge specified in the pattern.

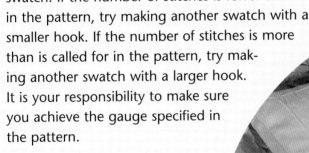

Fringe

Cut a piece of cardboard about 6" wide and half as long as specified in the instructions for strands, plus 1/2" for trimming allowance. Wind the thread loosely and evenly lengthwise around the cardboard. When the card is filled, cut the thread across one end. Do this several times; then begin fringing. You can wind additional strands as you need them.

1. Hold the specified number of strands for one knot of fringe together, and then fold in half.

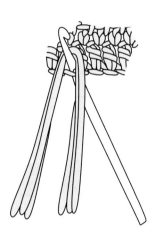

2. Hold the project with the right side facing you. Using a crochet hook, draw the folded ends through the space of stitch from right to wrong side.

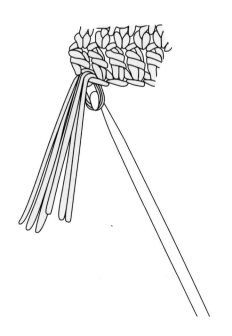

3. Pull the loose ends through the folded section.

4. Draw the knot up firmly.

Space the knots evenly and trim the ends of the fringe.

Metric Equivalents

inches	cm	inches	cm	inches	cm
1	2.54	11	27.94	21	53.34
2	5.08	12	30.48	22	55.88
3	7.62	13	33.02	23	58.42
4	10.16	14	35.56	24	60.96
5	12.70	15	38.10	30	76.20
6	15.24	16	40.64	36	91.44
7	17.78	17	43.18	42	106.68
8	20.32	18	45.72	48	121.92
9	22.86	19	48.26	54	137.16
10	25.40	20	50.8	60	152.40

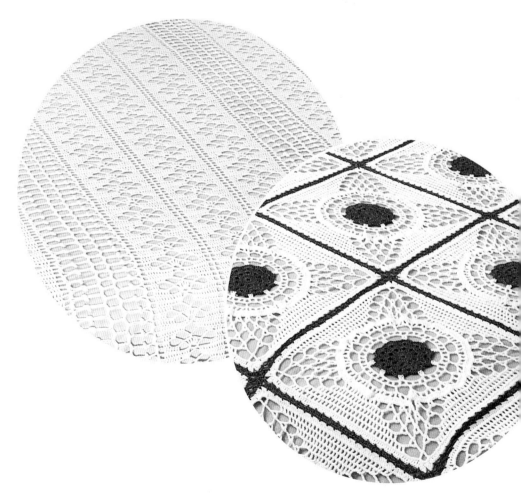

INDEX

Abbreviations, 139

Adjustable Size Pineapple Tablecloth, 106

Alphabet, 125

Angels, 94, 95

Animals, 95, 122-138

Animals on Parade Child's Spread, 120

Baskets, 12, 46

Bedspreads

    Animals on Parade Child's Spread, 120

    Elegance Bedspread. 70

    Filet Flower Baskets Bedroom Set, 42

    Floral Strips Bedspread, 52

    Frosty Pineapple Bedspread, 96

    Lacy Panels Bedspread, 18

    Peacock Filet Bedspread, 28

    Popcorn Diamonds Bedspread, 60

    Signs of Spring, 6

Birds, 9, 10, 32, 35, 128

Bunnies, 126, 127, 131

Butterfly, 115

Butterfly Filet Table Topper, 110

Cats, 128

Chickens, 129

Closed mesh, 136

Colorful Floral Squares, 56

Crochet thread, 133

Daisy Filigree Tablecloth, 86

Dog, 95, 129

Elegance Bedspread. 70

Elegance for the Table, 116

Elegant Pineapples Tablecloth, 22

Filet crochet, 134-138

Filet afghans, 6, 28, 42, 52, 66, 76, 90, 102, 110. 120

Filet Flower Baskets Bedroom Set, 42

Finishing, 133

Floral Medallions Tablecloth, 102

Floral Strips Bedspread, 52

Flower Circles Tablecloth, 48

Flowers, 11, 12, 13, 46, 54, 68, 69, 78, 79, 03, 105

Fringe, 142

Frosty Pineapple Bedspread, 96

Gauge, 141

God Bless Our Home Tablecloth, 66

Harvest Cloth, 90

International crochet terminology, 140

Lacets, 138

Lacy Panels Bedspread, 18

Numeals, 125

Open mesh, 136

Oval Filet Tablecloth, 76

Peacock, 32-35, 128

Peacock Filet Bedspread, 28

Pig, 131

Pineapple Ovals Tablecloth, 36

Popcorn Diamonds Bedspread, 60

Popcorns, 60-65

Rooster, 131

Rosy Table Topper, 80

Signs of Spring, 6

Spider Wheel Tablecloth, 14

Squirrel, 130

Stag, 130, 131

Steel hooks, 132

Swan, 1312

Symbols, 139

Tablecloths

    Adjustable Size Pineapple Tablecloth, 106

    Butterfly Filet Table Topper, 110

    Colorful Floral Squares, 56

    Daisy Filigree Tablecloth, 86

    Elegance for the Table, 116

    Elegant Pineapples Tablecloth, 22

    Floral Medallions Tablecloth, 102

    Flower Circles Tablecloth, 48

    God Bless Our Home Tablecloth, 66

    Harvest Cloth, 90

    Oval Filet Tablecloth, 76

    Pineapple Ovals Tablecloth, 36

    Rosy Table Topper, 80

    Spider Wheel Tablecloth, 14

Terms, 140